Retirement Planning: One Size Does Not Fit All

Optimize Time, Boost Income & Emergency Funds, Conquer Debt, Manage Budget, Investments, Health, Social Life, Retire Early, & Enjoy Leisure

A Holistic Essential Guide for Every Lifestyle!

For Beginners, Young Professionals, or Seasoned Retirees

Skylar Waves

By reading this document, the reader agrees that under no circumstances is the author or publisher responsible for any losses, direct or indirect, that are incurred as a result of the use of the information contained within this document, including, but not limited to, errors, omissions, or inaccuracies.

Dedication And Contact Information

First and foremost, I am extremely grateful to the Almighty God, the creator of our universe and everything in it, for all the blessings bestowed upon me. It is solely through His Divine Grace that I have been endowed with the profound knowledge, unwavering wisdom, and indomitable strength to craft this invaluable Guide.

With immense honor and humility, I share its insights with you, aspiring for its significance in your endeavors. This work is dedicated with heartfelt appreciation to my cherished family, steadfast friends, esteemed collaborators, and supportive readers. Without your encouragement and contributions, this creation would remain but a dream. From the depths of my heart, I extend my sincere gratitude as I could not have written this Guide without you.

For inquiries, please feel free to contact me at:

Skylar Waves
FlosRisingSun LLC
P. O. Box 1041
Woodbridge, VA 22195
Email: skylarthewaves@gmail.com

Skylar Waves
Publisher

Table of Contents

Introduction

Creating a robust retirement plan is a multifaceted endeavor, an intricate puzzle that doesn't offer a one-size-fits-all solution. Welcome to "Retirement Planning: One Size Does Not Fit All," an indispensable Guide crafted to navigate the diverse landscapes of retirement. As we embark on this journey, let's first explore the varied audiences who stand to gain invaluable insights from these pages.

Audiences

Retirement age varies from country to country, and also for individuals due to different backgrounds, location, social status, level of education, and the revolving economy among other factors; hence, one size does not fit all in the retirement planning process.

For example, in the United States of America (USA), individuals aged 65 years and older are considered retirees even though, technically, some may still be actively working. For other countries, the retirement age may be considered as 70 years and older, and this changes according to either the country's economy or the global economy as it frequently evolves.

The two most crucial pieces of information for individuals contemplating retirement in the near future are as follows:

(i) While it's never too late to begin planning for retirement, starting early allows you time to maximize benefits and potentially retire sooner; and (ii) it's essential to recognize that everyone's retirement journey is unique, and influenced by diverse backgrounds and circumstances. Comparing your situation to that of friends, colleagues, neighbors, or family members, even if you share similar employment histories, isn't a reliable roadmap. Each person's retirement plan should be tailored to their individual preferences and aspirations. There's no one-size-fits-all approach.

With this guide, we recommend taking a step-by-step approach, focusing on your own goals and desires to create a retirement plan that aligns perfectly with your dreams.

Once you have determined which of the eight bulleted categories below best describes you, we have got you covered throughout this great book:

- **Early Career Professionals:** These are professionals in their early career phases who are looking for proactive strategies to save for retirement.

- **Mid-career Individuals:** Those who are in the middle of their careers and are trying to optimize their savings and adjust their retirement plans.

- **Nearing Retirees:** People who are getting closer to retirement age and are ready to make a wish list of choices for a smooth transition.

- **Pre-retirees:** These folks are nearing retirement age and struggling with financial planning and asset allocation.

- **New Retirees:** Recently retired individuals who are acclimating to life after retirement and looking for guidance on using their newfound independence.

- **Active Retirees:** These individuals are already content in their retirement and are looking for methods to make the most of their assets and way of life.

- **Second-job Seekers:** Persons who, after retirement, are thinking about starting a second job or business.

- **Retirement Enthusiasts:** Regardless of their present employment level, these are people who are enthusiastic about learning more about retirement preparation.

Pain Points (Challenges Faced by Retirees)

This book will address and strive to ease the very dilemmas existing and new retirees face as they strive into a new life altogether:

- **Financial Insecurity:** Worries about whether or not they will have enough money to continue living the lifestyle they choose during their retirement years.

- **Healthcare Anxieties:** Worries about healthcare including the terrifying potential of escalating healthcare expenditures and the lack of certainty over proper medical coverage.

- **Market Volatility:** This is the fear of market changes affecting retirement savings and investments.

- **Lifestyle Adjustments:** Anxiety due to the process of changing to a new routine and finding one's purpose after quitting your profession can be daunting.

- **Obligations to the Family:** Striking a balance between providing financial assistance for family members and looking out for their retirement can often be a huge burden.

- **Longevity Concerns:** Uncertainty about outliving their assets and the financial ramifications of a longer life expectancy are two of the longest-lasting concerns.

- **Tax Implications:** Managing tax responsibilities properly and having a thorough understanding of the tax complexities involved in retirement planning can be intimidating.

- **Technology:** Managing the daily aspects of life using ever-evolving technology can be extremely difficult for seniors.

- **Connections:** Dealing with the loss of friends and family members who may have passed on, making and accepting new friends, and connecting with existing family members can be difficult.

- **Transportation:** Dealing with the fact that most retirees may not be able to drive due to various health issues and have to completely rely on family, friends, and public transportation can be stressful.

Benefits of This Book

These eight advantages are only a few of the many that may be gained by reading this book:

- **Tailored Strategies:** Strategies that are tailored to the specific needs of an individual, taking into consideration the various stages of their career as well as the preferences they have for their way of life.

- **Clarity Amidst Complexity:** To reduce sophisticated financial jargon and provide explanations that are easy to understand.

- **Comprehensive Insights:** This is the offering of a holistic view of retirement planning, which covers investments, healthcare, and estate planning.

- **Risk Mitigation:** Refers to the strategies that are undertaken to safeguard retirement assets against the unpredictability of the market and expenses that were not foreseen.

- **Empowerment by Knowledge:** Providing readers with the tactics and knowledge they need to make informed decisions based on factual facts that will empower them.

- **Practical Guidance:** Providing precise activities and checklists to aid the execution of a complete retirement plan. This type of information is also known as "practical guidance."

- **Professional Expertise:** This entails relying on the experiences of seasoned retirees and financial professionals to gain knowledge and insight into the real world.

- **Interactive Approach:** This involves incorporating activities and interactive components to encourage active engagement and make learning more efficient.

Additional Perks

A well-planned retirement should also allow you to enjoy worry-free perks such as:

- Creating the life you want.

- Go wherever you want to and when you want to.

- Make new friends with similar goals.

- Free yourself of your addiction to ambition.

- Allow you to still work part-time if need be, and you feel up to it.

- Keep current with your culture.

- Join a book club or other clubs, if desired.

- Babysit your grandchildren and bond with your family as you wish.

- Allow yourself the time and assets to give back to your society.

- Give yourself time to do nothing.

- Allow you to fully live your dream.

- Do what you have always wanted to do but couldn't.

Retiree Takeaways

For those who are retiring, keep the following eight points in mind:

- **Customized Planning:** Individualized planning is the preparation process of customizing retirement methods to the particular lifestyles and aspirations of each individual.

- **Diverse Investment Methods:** One of the many different investing methods is doing research on a wide range of investment alternatives and analyzing the impact that these choices have on retirement portfolios.

- **Healthcare Optimization:** To manage one's healthcare alternatives and become aware of how those decisions will impact one's retirement savings or financial situation.

- **Risk Management:** Comprised of the use of risk reduction strategies to protect retirement savings throughout retirement.

- **Lifestyle Design:** The process of building habits and activities that you like to create a meaningful existence for yourself after retirement.

- **The Process of Financial Planning for the Family:** This process requires striking a balance between the responsibility of giving help to family members and the pursuit of personal retirement goals.

- **Longevity Preparations:** The category of long-term preparations consists of strategies that may be used to provide financial stability even throughout the extended retirement years.

- **Tax-efficient Planning:** It is necessary to be aware of the impacts of taxes and to optimize retirement plans for those consequences.

To begin the path toward achieving financial stability and a life that is enjoyable after retirement, it is necessary to have a thorough grasp of one's specific requirements, objectives, and preferences within the complex framework of retirement planning. The purpose of this all-encompassing book is to shed light on the way ahead by providing individualized guidance and real-world application to successfully traverse the complex maze of retirement planning.

Steps Into Your Golden Years One Page at a Time

This book invites you to go on an illuminating trip that goes beyond the traditional bounds of retirement planning. This vital book reveals and simplifies the complexities involved in developing a solid retirement plan, recognizing that it is more than simply a financial puzzle; rather, it is a tapestry that is woven with many threads of health, purpose, relationships, and personal development. As you read through these pages, you will dig into the many landscapes of retirement and uncover essential insights geared toward a wide variety of audiences.

If you are looking for a dynamic post-career life, if you want to retain your health and well-being, or if you want to leave a legacy that will survive for generations, this book is the compass that will guide you through the course of your journey. We ask you to join us as we uncover the secrets to constructing a retirement that is both meaningful and purpose-driven. Each page of this book encourages you to explore, learn, and chart your unique route to a life that is rewarding after you have retired from your profession. Start your path toward your individualized retirement plan by turning the first page of this book and embarking on a revolutionary adventure.

Transition: Come along with me as we go on an exciting trip, and together, we will discover the three most important questions that will start your journey toward retirement planning in no time.

Chapter 1: The Three Big Retirement Questions

The Three Key Questions

In the world of retirement planning, three important questions need to be addressed. They are crucial for ensuring a fulfilling and secure future during your golden years. These questions are:

(1) When will I have enough money to retire?

(2) Where should I live?

(3) How will I spend my time?

Each question represents a chapter in the story of retirement, highlighting the key aspects of a satisfying post-career life. From financial security and lifestyle choices to pursuing passions, these questions delve into the heart of a rewarding retirement.

In the upcoming chapters, we will carefully examine these questions, drawing insights from experts, data-driven analyses, and practical wisdom. We will navigate through these important considerations to pave the way for a vibrant retirement by exploring topics such as financial preparedness, housing options, and various ways to enrich your post-retirement life.

As we delve deeper into each question, remember the words of Anna Marion Hilliard, a Canadian Physician, who captured the essence of retirement as "a new adventure in living—not a stopping." Retirement is not about pausing or ending your way of life but it's rather about embracing, fulfilling, and enriching your future.

Stay tuned for a comprehensive exploration that will shed light on these questions, helping you create a retirement that is not just about ceasing work but about embracing a life filled with purpose and enjoyment.

Determining the ideal monthly income for retirement is a crucial part of retirement planning. According to articles by The Motley Fool and Discovery, a common guideline suggests aiming for about 80 percent of your pre-retirement monthly income. To estimate your monthly income needs, a simple calculation is recommended:

Calculate 80 percent of your pre-retirement monthly income.

And 20 percent from Social Security, home equities, family inheritances, or from other sources that may be available to you, etc.

- For example, if your current yearly income is $100,000, aiming for $80,000 annually would be the goal.

- To convert this yearly estimate into a monthly figure, divide $80,000 by 12 months:

$80,000 / 12 = $6,667.

$20,000/12 = $1,667.

Estimated monthly income needed = $8,334.

This approach suggests adjusting your retirement savings annually to align with your current income. This allows for potential lifestyle changes or income fluctuations over the years, ensuring that your savings are in line with your evolving circumstances.

It is important to note that this estimate is not universally applicable. The actual amount needed for retirement can vary based on your specific retirement plans. For example, an extravagant retirement with extensive travel might require an income exceeding the 80 percent benchmark, while a more modest retirement with fewer expenses might necessitate a lower income threshold.

Therefore, while the 80 percent guideline is a useful starting point, it is important to consider your individual retirement aspirations. Regularly reassessing your retirement savings strategies, taking into account your evolving lifestyle goals and financial capabilities, will ensure that your savings align with your envisioned retirement lifestyle.

In fact, most people do not have enough savings to retire but with careful and early planning, a golden retirement is achievable and it is not as difficult as you think. So, do not worry as we will show you in the next few chapters, how you too can plan your golden retirement. But first, let's look at Harold's story.

A Story: Harold's Journey to Answering the Three Big Retirement Questions

Let's meet Harold Smith, a cheerful man with a contagious laugh and a deep love for his job. Retirement seemed like a distant dream as he threw himself into his work, believing that he would have enough saved when the time came. But as the years went by, reality hit harder than he expected.

When Harold retired, he had very little in savings and relied heavily on Social Security to get by. At first, it felt like a relief to escape the daily grind, but soon, he found himself struggling to cover mounting bills with his fixed income. Social Security was not enough to meet his needs.

Every day became a challenge to make ends meet. Harold tried to find part-time work, but opportunities for an aging retiree were scarce during his time. He found himself trapped in a cycle of working low-paying jobs just to scrape by. Retirement, which was once a promise of relaxation, now felt like an endless struggle.

The dreams of leisurely days and pursuing his passions slowly faded into a distant memory. Harold longed to travel and indulge in the activities he had put aside during his working years. But exhaustion clouded his desires. He had to work, no matter how old or tired he felt.

In moments of reflection, Harold wished for a different path—a life where he had financial security and could actively engage in the activities he had always yearned for. He wished he could convey to others the importance of planning for retirement, not just for survival but for the freedom to truly enjoy life without financial burdens.

So, Harold's story stands as a plea, a call to action. Consider the alternative, where diligent planning allows for a financially secure retirement. Imagine a life where you have the time and resources to pursue the activities that currently take a back seat amidst the daily grind.

Harold's tale is a reminder that relying solely on Social Security won't create a blissful retirement. It is a plea to start planning today for a future where your golden years are truly golden, filled with the joys and experiences that make life worth living.

Choosing the Perfect Place to Retire: Factors to Consider

When deciding where to spend your retirement years, there are several important factors to consider. Insights from experts, including Investopedia, Retire Successfully, and Apprise Wealth Management, shed light on the key considerations to ponder:

- **Moving Costs and New Expenses:** Relocating comes with its own set of expenses, including the cost of setting up a new household, such as purchasing furniture or making renovations.

- **Cost of Living in the New Location:** The cost of living varies widely in different areas. Evaluate and research multiple locations for the cost of housing, groceries, healthcare, and other essentials in potential locations to ensure they align with your retirement budget.

- **Proximity to Family and Friends:** Being close to loved ones can greatly enhance your retirement experience, providing peace of mind, important support, companionship, and shared joyful experiences.

- **Climate, Social Life, and Healthcare Facilities:** Consider factors such as the climate that suits your preferences, the availability of social activities, and the proximity to quality healthcare facilities for easy access to medical care as you age. Thoughtfully assessing and weighing these factors will enable you to make an informed decision about the ideal location to call home during your retirement years.

A Story: Choosing Retirement Destinations

Let's meet Ellie and Sam Johnson, a couple who have always cherished their cozy family home. However, as retirement approached, they saw an opportunity for a new beginning. Downsizing felt liberating—a chance to let go of unnecessary space and responsibilities. They happily said goodbye to the empty rooms and large yard, opting for a smaller, low-maintenance cottage.

This move opened up a world of possibilities. Ellie and Sam embraced the simplicity of their smaller space, spending less time on maintenance and more on the activities they enjoyed. They attended local events, explored new hobbies, and cherished impromptu adventures. Downsizing brought them closer together, fostering a sense of togetherness that their larger home had sometimes overshadowed.

On the other side of town, Helen and David were reveling in their decision to relocate to a warmer climate. The sun-filled days and pleasant weather felt like a warm embrace, soothing their bodies and lifting their spirits. They marveled at the beauty of each sunset, wishing they had made the move sooner. The community welcomed them with open arms, and they immersed themselves in a lifestyle filled with outdoor activities and new friendships.

Meanwhile, just a few streets away, Sarah Rockson found immense joy in staying right where she was. As a single retiree, her modest house was her haven. It was conveniently close to her grandchildren, allowing her to be their doting babysitter. She cherished the laughter that filled her home and the moments spent sharing stories and secrets with her beloved grandkids. For Sarah, being near her family was the ultimate source of contentment.

These diverse retirement stories paint a vivid picture—the beauty of personalized happiness. For Ellie and Sam, downsizing brought freedom; for Helen and David, relocating brought newfound joy; and for Sarah, staying close to family was priceless. It is a reminder that retirement is not a one-size-fits-all deal. It's about finding a path that aligns with your personal priorities and brings contentment and fulfillment in unique ways to you. *What truly matters is finding your own formula for happiness in this new chapter of your life.*

Crafting a Fulfilling Retirement: Planning and Pursuits

Planning Ahead for Retirement—Laying the Foundation: Retirement isn't just a milestone; it's a new chapter waiting to be written. According to Nolo's insights, it's important to start this journey early by visualizing and planning your post-career life. *By beginning the process before retirement, you can map out goals, aspirations, and financial strategies, which will make for a smoother and more fulfilling transition.*

Part-Time Engagement Embracing Opportunities Beyond Full Retirement: When it comes to retirement, part-time work shouldn't be overlooked. Nolo emphasizes that it's not just about supplementing income but also about staying connected and engaged. Part-time employment can provide avenues to pursue your passions, mentor others, or explore new career paths. It offers structure, social interaction, and flexibility in your schedule.

Volunteerism—Contributing Meaningfully Beyond Retirement: Volunteering is another meaningful way to spend your retirement years, as highlighted by Nolo. It goes beyond personal gratification and allows you to use your skills and experiences to make a difference in society. Contributing to meaningful causes can bring a sense of fulfillment and societal impact, enhancing your retirement experience.

Exploring Hobbies—Enriching Retirement with Personal Pursuits: Esimoney emphasizes the significance of hobbies in retirement. Retirement provides the time and freedom to delve into interests that you may have put off in the past. Whether it's pursuing artistic endeavors, engaging in outdoor activities, or diving into intellectual pursuits, hobbies can bring joy, learning, and personal enrichment to your retired years.

Crafting a Purposeful Retirement—Structuring Time and Activities: According to Wharton Knowledge, planning is crucial for a fulfilling retirement. It's not just about escaping the traditional work routine; it's about envisioning and structuring a life that excites and fulfills you. Retirement offers an opportunity for purposeful pursuits, exploring diverse interests, and engaging in meaningful activities that align with your individual fulfillment and happiness.

Retirement isn't a one-size-fits-all journey. By starting planning early, considering part-time work or volunteering, exploring hobbies, and structuring your time and activities, you can curate a retirement that is tailored to your personal aspirations. *Each chapter of retirement contributes to a richer, more purposeful life, emphasizing that the true essence of retirement lies in pursuing what brings you contentment and happiness.*

A Story: Retirement's Canvas: Embracing Vibrancy in Every Stroke

In a quiet neighborhood, two retirees, Emily Everton and Jack Richardson, lived next to each other but experienced retirement in different ways. Their experiences showcased the range of possibilities in this phase of life.

Emily found herself feeling bored and unfulfilled in retirement. Her days became monotonous, lacking purpose and excitement. She felt her once-vibrant spirit dimmed by the absence of engaging activities. Retirement, to her disappointment, felt mundane and lacked the zest she had imagined.

On the other hand, Jack embraced retirement with vitality and purpose. He engaged in various activities that made him feel alive. Volunteering at a local shelter brought warmth and fulfillment to his heart, connecting him with a community beyond retirement. Socializing became a daily ritual, where he shared laughter and stories with old and new friends. Regular exercise sessions kept him physically fit and invigorated.

Jack's enthusiasm extended to his side hustle of repairing cars. It wasn't just about the income; it was a passion that provided intellectual stimulation and a sense of achievement. He also found solace in nature, spending time outside and enjoying the tranquility of the surroundings.

Their contrasting experiences revealed an essential truth: retirement offers a diverse and ever-evolving canvas. Emily's struggle highlighted the importance of planning how to spend your time after your career. Jack's vibrant lifestyle showed the freedom to mold and reshape retirement activities based on personal preferences and evolving interests.

The key takeaway was that retirement plans should be flexible roadmaps that guide your journey. *The key is to find a reason to wake up each morning, embrace activities that fuel your soul, and stay active. It's not about rigid schedules, but about remaining engaged, invigorated, and having the freedom to switch gears and pursue new passions.*

In their neighborhood, Jack became an inspiration for others, showing them the limitless possibilities retirement offers. He encouraged them to see this chapter of life as an ever-evolving adventure where the only constant is the joy of staying active and engaged.

The takeaway message is that retirement is a blank canvas waiting for purpose and activity. It invites individuals to craft a life filled with vitality, passion, and fulfillment, knowing that plans can change as often as needed to keep the excitement alive.

Retirement Readiness: Your Three-Step Journey to Planning and Purpose

Here's a suggestion for readers to start thinking about their retirement plans:

Step 1: Assess Your Financial Outlook

- Calculate 80 percent of your current salary to estimate your retirement income goal. Example: If your current salary is $60,000, 80 percent is $48,000 annually.

- Determine 5 percent of your current retirement savings to understand its contribution. For example, if you have $150,000 saved, 5 percent is $7,500.

- Estimate your potential Social Security income using online calculators or rough estimates based on your earnings history.

- Calculate the projected shortfall in retirement income. Example Calculation: ($48,000 - $7,500 - Estimated Social Security) = Annual Shortfall.

- Divide the annual shortfall by 12 to understand the monthly deficit.

Step 2: Consider Your Retirement Location

- Make a list of the pros and cons of staying in your current location versus moving. Consider factors such as cost of living, proximity to family and friends, climate, healthcare facilities, and social life.

- Evaluate the impact of moving on your lifestyle and expenses. Think about how a new location could align with your retirement goals and desires.

Step 3: Plan Your Retirement Activities

- Start thinking about and writing down activities or interests you wish to pursue in retirement.

- Encourage flexibility in your retirement plans. Write down multiple activities or hobbies to ensure a diverse and fulfilling retirement. *Emphasize that while one goal may be appealing, it may not guarantee lasting fulfillment, and it's okay to revisit and adapt your plans over time.*

Transition: In the next chapter, we will learn more about money-saving tips in financial foundation and budgeting. During the next few pages, we will discover how to budget our funds, prioritize our spending by using delay gratification, build an emergency fund, and reduce debt.

Chapter 2: Financial Foundation— Budgeting

Budgeting is not just for people who do not have enough money. It is for everyone who wants to ensure that their money is enough.–Rosette Mugidde Wamambe.

Needs and Wants

Understanding the difference between needs and wants is essential for effective financial management. According to Fairwinds Credit Union (n.d.), needs are the basic elements necessary for survival and well-being, such as shelter, food, clothing, healthcare, education, and transportation. These are fundamental requirements that sustain life and enable basic functioning in society. Balance Money (n.d.) reinforces this idea, stating that needs are crucial for maintaining a reasonable standard of living and are non-negotiable for personal health and safety.

On the other hand, wants, as described by FI Money (n.d.), are desires beyond the necessities of life. These desires often focus on leisure, entertainment, and indulgence, such as vacations, the latest gadgets, trendy clothes, dining out, luxury items, and hobbies. Wants are not necessary for survival but contribute to enjoyment, pleasure, and lifestyle enhancement.

It is important to note that recognizing the difference between needs and wants does not mean completely depriving oneself of life's pleasures. Instead, it encourages mindful spending and self-reflection. Budgeting involves consciously evaluating expenditures on wants and understanding their value in bringing happiness and satisfaction.

The 50/30/20 rule, mentioned by The Balance Money (n.d.), serves as a guideline for balancing needs and wants within a budget. This rule suggests allocating 50 percent of income to needs, 30 percent to wants, and 20 percent to savings and debt repayment. This allocation strategy empowers individuals to prioritize needs while still allowing for discretionary spending on wants, ensuring a balance between financial stability and enjoying life's pleasures.

Ultimately, the goal is not to sacrifice all enjoyable aspects of life but to make informed choices about spending. It is about aligning expenditures with personal values and goals, ensuring that you want to contribute meaningfully to happiness and fulfillment without jeopardizing financial security.

A Story: Riches Reimagined—The Tale of Extravagance and Altruism

Once upon a time, Johnny Depp and Bill Gates lived lavishly and dreamed big. Their tales showed how tremendous prosperity can go two ways.

Johnny Depp, the mysterious Hollywood Actor, wowed audiences with his performance and spending habits. The world gasped at Johnny's opulent lifestyle, where spending $2 million a month was routine, and was revealed. His love of luxury was endless, from private islands and estates, to collections, and vehicles. Despite the sparkle and splendor, there appeared to be a hole.

While the public admired Johnny's extravagance, Bill Gates' story was quite different. Bill had financial power and a deep sense of duty as a Microsoft Co-founder. Bill used his money for non-material causes in a world where wealth could buy anything. According to the Los Angeles Times, he donated $5 billion in 2022, demonstrating his love for charity and worldwide goodwill.

The difference between these two rich people makes one question money. Johnny's biography shows how even great wealth may fall prey to self-indulgence and excess. Where is the actual treasure of satisfaction and purpose among the glamour?

However, Bill represents charity and influence. His philanthropy shows how money may benefit society. Hope, transformation, and real answers to global issues were represented by the $5 billion gift.

Their tales remind us of money and power. *Wealth requires management, not just accumulation. It is about using privilege to improve lives and make a difference.*

The anecdote illustrates a basic truth: *money is worth more for its legacy than its riches.* Impact on the globe, lives changed, and differences made for a better future. *The ultimate measure of riches is what one gives back.*

Johnny and Bill's tales resound with a fundamental decision in the hallways of riches, where splendor and kindness meet. This option transcends wealth and touches on human values and purpose.

Impulse Spending

Uncontrolled impulse spending can have a significant impact on long-term financial stability and retirement plans. Here is how these factors are interconnected:

- **Delayed Gratification:** This involves resisting the temptation of an immediate reward to achieve a better outcome in the future. It is the ability to wait for something you want, sacrificing instant pleasure for a more significant long-term benefit, such as saving for retirement.

- **Emotional Triggers:** Emotional triggers often lead to impulse spending. Feelings of stress, boredom, or social pressures can push individuals into making spontaneous purchases. *Recognizing these triggers is crucial for gaining control over impulsive buying habits.*

- **Shopping List Discipline:** Creating and sticking to a shopping list helps curb impulsive purchases. By planning what you need ahead of time, you are less likely to deviate from the list and buy items on a whim.

- **Non-materialistic Alternatives:** Finding non-materialistic ways to fulfill desires or cope with emotions can redirect spending impulses. Engaging in hobbies, exercising, or spending time with loved ones can provide fulfillment without the need for excessive spending.

- **The 24-hour Rule:** The 24-hour rule is a strategy that involves waiting at least a day before making a non-essential purchase. It allows time to reconsider the necessity and impact of the purchase, reducing impulsive buying. This cooling-off period promotes a more rational decision-making process.

- **Impact on Retirement and Financial Stability:** *Uncontrolled impulse spending directly affects saving and investing capacity.* Continuously spending on non-essential items reduces the amount of money available for retirement savings. By curbing impulsive purchases, individuals can redirect those funds towards investments or retirement accounts, potentially accelerating their retirement timeline and ensuring a more comfortable retirement.

- **Influence of Social Media:** Social media can amplify impulse spending by showcasing idealized lifestyles and products. Being aware of these influences can help individuals differentiate between genuine needs and the desire to keep up with trends, ultimately aiding in controlling impulsive spending.

By understanding delayed gratification, recognizing emotional triggers, adhering to shopping lists, exploring non-materialistic satisfaction, and employing the 24-hour rule, individuals can regain control over impulse spending. This control directly contributes to improved financial stability and a more secure retirement.

A Story: Beyond Impulse—A Journey from Spree to Serenity

The flourishing city of Cascade once had a young lady called Lily Becker. Her pals knew she could convert any window shopping excursion into an impromptu frenzy. Her wardrobe was full of stylish clothing with tags, her shelves were full of technology she seldom used, and her credit card bills were worrying.

In the past, Lily started differently. She learned money management and saving from her thrifty parents. As she became an adult and got her first job, bright new objects pulled her in. Every day after work, she browsed malls for bargains   and   discounts. Impulsive shopping crept into her life. Lily struggled to make her payments; her savings account decreased, and tension increased. She struggled financially but she couldn't resist the fleeting joy of each purchase.

Lily accidentally found a r/Anticonsumption (n.d.) discussion while aimlessly reading Reddit. Storytelling about impulsive purchases moved her. She saw she wasn't alone in her battle and resolved to change.

Lily began her redemption after reading subreddit debates and recommendations. Her buying habits were extensively examined to determine impulsive purchase triggers. Shopping became her escape from stress and boredom.

Lily used her newfound understanding to control her urges. She began keeping a notebook to record her shopping urges. She gradually became better at stress management by doing yoga and volunteering at an animal shelter. She managed to return some of the items that were not too late to return to the stores. Every time she did this, a big smile came to her face as she recovered some of her money.

Lily learned about budgeting and personal finance via r/IWantToLearn (n.d.). She planned a thorough budget for needs and a tiny allowance for treats. Her most significant transformation came from the 24-hour rule, a simple yet profound guideline.

Implementing the 24-hour regulation changed Lily's game. When she felt tempted to buy anything impulsively, she would move away and think about it later. Her initial urge usually faded, and she realized it wasn't worth risking her financial security.

Lily changed over the months. Her credit card expenses dropped, her savings account expanded, and she felt empowered instead of guilty and stressed. She valued time with family and friends which was not only enjoyable but also prevented her from her impulsive purchases.

Lily overcame compulsive purchases with hard work. She publicly documented her story on the same Reddit posts that motivated her, supporting others in similar challenges.

Lily beamed at her orderly closet full of treasures. She cannot believe that she made it. Her tale showed how self-awareness, resilience, and how a supportive online network helped her. She recovered financial control and found serenity and satisfaction.

Necessity of Tracking Expenses

In today's ever-changing financial landscape, tracking expenses is not just a good practice but an essential tool for maintaining financial health and achieving monetary goals (NerdWallet, n.d.). By meticulously recording and evaluating every expenditure, individuals gain insight into their financial behaviors, which leads to informed decision-making and improved financial management.

Maintain Detailed Records: *Accurate and comprehensive records are the foundation of effective expense tracking.* Keeping a detailed log of all transactions, big or small, provides a clear view of spending patterns (NerdWallet, n.d.). From monthly bills to impulsive purchases, *every expense should be recorded*, fostering an understanding of where money is going and why?

Utilize Budgeting Apps: Technology has revolutionized expense tracking, offering a wide range of budgeting apps tailored to different needs and preferences (Clockify, n.d.). Popular apps like Mint, YNAB (You Need a Budget), and PocketGuard provide user-friendly interfaces and functionalities (Intuit Mint, n.d.). These tools sync with bank accounts, categorize expenses, and offer real-time insights into spending habits, streamlining the tracking process.

Identify Areas for Optimization: Through careful tracking, individuals can identify areas where spending can be optimized or reduced (Take Charge America, n.d.). These insights reveal patterns of unnecessary expenses, helping to create strategies to cut back on non-essential spending. For example, discovering subscriptions or services that are rarely used can prompt cancellation, freeing up funds for more meaningful purposes.

Regular Habit Formation: Consistency is key to successful expense tracking (Money View, n.d.). Making it a regular habit, preferably on a daily or weekly basis, ensures that no expense goes unnoticed. Incorporating tracking into a routine transforms it from a sporadic task into a natural part of financial management. Over time, this habit fosters greater financial mindfulness and accountability.

Expense tracking is not just about recording transactions; it is a proactive approach to financial well-being. Through meticulous record-keeping, the use of budgeting apps, identifying optimization opportunities, and forming a regular tracking habit, individuals can gain control over their finances. This practice empowers informed decision-making, facilitates budgeting, and helps individuals achieve their financial goals.

Importance of an Emergency Fund

Undoubtedly, an emergency fund serves as a crucial financial safety net, as emphasized by various sources such as NerdWallet, Investopedia, and Willful.

Avoiding High-Interest Debt: *One of the primary advantages of having an emergency fund is its ability to prevent individuals from falling into high-interest debt during unexpected expenses* (NerdWallet, n.d.). These unforeseen situations could range from medical emergencies to car repairs or job losses. Without an emergency fund, people might resort to credit cards or loans with steep interest rates, further exacerbating their financial stress (Investopedia, n.d.).

Reducing Financial Stress: By maintaining an emergency fund, individuals can alleviate the financial stress caused by unexpected events (Willful, n.d.). *Having readily accessible funds specifically designated for emergencies provides a sense of security and peace of mind.* This financial cushion allows individuals to navigate crises without jeopardizing their long-term financial goals or resorting to debt.

Recommended Fund Size: Three to Six Months of Living Expenses: *Financial experts generally recommend that an emergency fund should ideally cover three to six months of living expenses* (Investopedia, n.d.). This buffer enables individuals to sustain their lifestyle and cover essential costs in the event of job loss or unforeseen circumstances. However, the specific fund size can vary depending on individual circumstances such as employment stability, family size, and industry volatility.

An emergency fund acts as a crucial tool for maintaining financial stability. It safeguards against high-interest debt, ensuring that unexpected expenses or emergencies do not derail long-term financial goals. By adhering to the advice of covering three to six months of living expenses, individuals can establish a solid financial foundation, reduce stress, and foster resilience in the face of unpredicted events.

Simplicity of the 50/30/20 Rule

The 50/30/20 rule provides a simple and intuitive approach to budgeting, dividing income into three distinct categories: needs, wants, and savings, as explained by NerdWallet, N26, and Britannica.

- **Needs (50 percent of Income):** The beauty of this rule lies in its simplicity. It designates 50 percent of your income to cover essential needs such as housing, utilities, groceries, transportation, and other unavoidable expenses (NerdWallet, n.d.). This portion ensures that your basic requirements are met without stretching your budget too thin.

- **Wants (30 percent of Income):** The rule allocates 30 percent of income to discretionary spending or wants, which include non-essential expenses like dining out, entertainment, hobbies, and luxuries (N26, n.d.). This category allows for some flexibility and enjoyment without compromising financial stability.

- **Savings (20 percent of Income, after Debt Payments):** The remaining 20 percent is dedicated to savings and debt payments (Britannica, n.d.). *However, it is advisable to prioritize debt repayment before allocating funds to savings.* This portion contributes to building an emergency fund, retirement savings, investments, or paying off outstanding debts, ensuring a secure financial future.

Retirement Savings: 10 to 15 Percent Rule of Thumb

While the 50/30/20 rule covers general savings, a rule of thumb for retirement savings suggests setting aside 10 to 15 percent of your income (TIAA, n.d.). However, this allocation can vary based on individual circumstances, such as age, years until retirement, and financial goals (NerdWallet, n.d.).

Rest assured, Chapter 4 will explore the specifics of retirement savings and explain how to tailor these savings based on your unique circumstances and goals. It will discuss strategies to optimize retirement savings while balancing other financial priorities. By following the 50/30/20 rule and adjusting retirement savings based on individual factors, individuals can achieve a well-rounded financial plan that caters to both immediate needs and long-term security.

Good Debt Versus Bad Debt

Let's explore the differences between good and bad debt, the negative impacts of excessive bad debt on future financial stability, and strategies to effectively reduce debt based on the sources provided.

- **Good Debt:** Good debt typically refers to borrowing that is used for investments that have the potential to increase in value or generate income over time (Debt.org, n.d.). Examples of good debt include student loans for education, mortgages for property investments, or business loans for entrepreneurship (Britannica, n.d.). These types of debts can potentially lead to positive financial outcomes and asset accumulation.

- **Bad Debt:** In contrast, bad debt involves borrowing for items or services that do not appreciate or generate long-term income. Examples of bad debt include high-interest credit card debt for non-essential purchases or payday loans (Debt.org, n.d.). Bad debt often accrues high-interest rates, leading to financial strain and negatively impacting overall financial health (Britannica, n.d.).

The Negative Effects of Too Much Bad Debt

Accumulating excessive bad debt can severely hinder future financial stability. It leads to high-interest payments, reducing disposable income for savings or investments (The Balance Money, n.d.). It can negatively impact credit scores, making it challenging to secure favorable loan terms for future endeavors (Experian, n.d.).

Ultimately, it limits financial flexibility and can impede long-term wealth-building opportunities.

Strategies to Reduce Debt

- **Create a Budget and Payment Plan:** Develop a comprehensive budget to understand income, expenses, and debt obligations. Establish a repayment plan by prioritizing high-interest debts while making minimum payments on all others.

- **Snowball or Avalanche Method:** Consider debt repayment strategies like the snowball or avalanche method. The snowball method involves paying off the smallest debt first, gaining momentum, while the avalanche method focuses on high-interest debts to minimize overall interest payments.

- **Debt Consolidation:** Consolidate debts with high-interest rates into a single, lower-interest loan or through balance transfers to reduce interest payments and streamline repayments.

- **Increase Income and Cut Expenses:** Explore ways to increase income through side hustles or additional work. Simultaneously, cut unnecessary expenses to allocate more funds toward debt repayment (Lendified, n.d.).

By understanding the difference between good and bad debt, acknowledging the detrimental effects of excessive bad debt, and implementing effective debt reduction strategies, individuals can gradually regain financial stability and work towards a debt-free future.

A Story: Debt to Freedom—The Journey of Building an Emergency Fund

Emma Hughes, Jack Addy, and Maya Robinson were close friends in a busy metropolis. They laughed, dreamed, and worried about money together. Each had pursued their occupations with enthusiasm and drive, but financial issues left them with increasing bills and depleted emergency accounts.

Student loans and credit card bills appeared overwhelming for Emma, a young marketing professional. Due to unanticipated medical expenditures and overspending, Jack, a dedicated IT professional, was in debt. A failing company left Maya, a determined businesswoman, drowning in debt.

Once exciting and full of hope, their chats became late-night debates about bills, debts, and the battle to make ends meet. One of these Reddit threads talks about optimism.

They found accounts on r/CalebHammer of people who had overcome financial hardship by prioritizing debt reduction and emergency money. These stories inspired Emma, Jack, and Maya to make a financial deal to pay off their debts.

Eventually, they actively paid off their debts and saved for emergencies. They carefully planned budgets, eliminated needless spending, and found freelance or side jobs to supplement their income.

The voyage was hard. It took sacrifices and avoiding temptations not to deviate. But Emma, Jack, and Maya persevered. They patiently kept chipping off their bills, encouraging, reminding, and aiding one another when temptation struck while building their emergency reserves.

Progress was slow but steady. Small debt reduction wins strengthened their drive. Growing emergency money gave them security, comfort, and peace of mind. They took comfort in knowing they were developing a financial buffer against life's risks.

Year after year, finally, their perseverance paid off. Emma, Jack, and Maya celebrated debt payback milestones. Once small emergency savings have evolved into strong safety nets, offering stability and trust.

With their debts paid and their emergency reserves growing, they felt free and optimistic. This lifted weights off their shoulders and gave them a better financial outlook. Their future appears better now, but they didn't lose sight. They supported each other and developed their fortunes. Knowing how they felt whilst in debt, they promised each other that they would try never to be in debt again. They toasted to this with a cheap glass of wine one evening while chatting about old times. They kept doing whatever additional job they could find, supporting each other and avoiding unnecessary expenditures. They don't want to work their whole lives, but they know that overspending is the one thing they can manage to prevent debt, so they made this their lifelong aim.

United by their victories, they shared their tales on the forum that had triggered their change to encourage others facing similar challenges. Their story showed strength, tenacity, camaraderie, and the transformational potential of financial health.

Emma, Jack, and Maya emerged debt-free, confident, and ready to face a bright future with the security of their emergency reserves.

Interactive Exercise

Let's delve deeper into the interactive elements, providing more detail and guidance for readers:

Expense Analysis

Categorizing Expenses: Take the time to meticulously review your credit card and bank statements from the past three months. Categorize your expenses into two primary groups: Needs and Wants.

- **Needs:** These are essential expenses for survival and maintaining your livelihood, such as rent/mortgage, utilities, groceries, transportation, insurance, and minimum debt payments.

- **Wants:** Identify non-essential expenses that contribute to lifestyle choices and leisure activities, such as dining out, entertainment, subscriptions, shopping for non-essential items, and hobbies.

- **Reflecting on Wants:** As you analyze your "wants," consider their significance in your life. *Ask yourself how many of these expenses genuinely bring joy, fulfillment, or long-term value. Reflect on whether these purchases align with your values and contribute positively to your overall well-being.*

Identifying Savings Opportunities: Look for areas where you could potentially cut back or save money:

- **Expired Items:** Check expiration dates on products at your local store before you purchase them to provide you with a longer shelf life. Also, check your pantry and fridge for expired items that could lead to waste and unnecessary spending. *Use the first-in, first-out inventory method (FIFO).* This generally means that products are used in the sequence in which they are purchased making sure that you are not throwing away products purchased with your hard-earned money, or getting sick from eating expired foods that could potentially cost you through sickness and hospital bills.

- **Shopping Habits:** Assess whether you always shop at the most expensive stores or if there are opportunities to explore more budget-friendly options or sales.

- **Unused Memberships:** Evaluate memberships or subscriptions (like gym memberships or streaming services) that you hardly use. Consider canceling or downgrading those that don't add significant value to your life.

Creating a Budget

Using Tools for Budgeting: Consider utilizing budgeting apps like Mint, YNAB, PocketGuard, or creating a spreadsheet to structure your budget. Input your categorized expenses, allocate funds for needs, and set aside a reasonable amount for wants based on your analysis.

- **Allocating Funds:** Ensure that your budget reflects your priorities and financial goals. Allocate funds for savings, debt repayment, and emergencies within your means.

Additional Note

- **Income Boosting:** If you find it challenging to create a balanced budget, know that exploring opportunities to increase your income will be covered in the following chapter. This step isn't a cause for worry but an opportunity for improvement.

Remember, this exercise aims to empower you with a clearer understanding of your spending habits and financial priorities. It's a pivotal step toward responsible financial management and setting the stage for informed budgeting and improved financial wellness.

Transition: Say goodbye to retirement worries and hello to a vibrant future. In the upcoming chapter, discover the smart, easy, and fun secrets to turn your spare time into exciting side hustles. Get ready to transform your retirement journey—let's dive in!

Chapter 3: Turning Spare Time Into Cash

Embracing Side Hustles for Financial Growth

For those who are planning for retirement or are already retired, let's take a closer look at the stories of Sophia Amoruso, Rob and Melissa Stephenson, and Brian Winch as examples by highlighting their side hustle journeys that turned their passions into profitable ventures:

Sophia Amoruso—Founder of Nasty Gal: Sophia's story is a perfect example of how a hobby can be transformed into a successful business empire. She started by selling vintage clothes on eBay, leveraging her keen eye for fashion and her passion for unique styles to create Nasty Gal, a renowned fashion brand.

- **Journey Highlights—Passion for Fashion:** Sophia's fascination with vintage clothing and her knack for finding unique pieces inspired her eBay store. Her understanding of customer preferences and trends helped her build her fashion empire.

- **Entrepreneurial Spirit:** Recognizing the potential of her side hustle, Sophia went on to found Nasty Gal and achieved success due to her innovative marketing strategies and dedication.

Rob and Melissa Stephenson—Bloggers at Flea Market Flipper: Rob and Melissa's journey started with their shared interest in flipping items for profit. They had a passion for finding undervalued items in thrift stores and reselling them for a higher price, which eventually led to the creation of their successful blog, Flea Market Flipper.

- **Journey Highlights—Thrift Store Expertise:** Rob and Melissa honed their skills by identifying valuable items in thrift stores and flipping them for a profit. Their knowledge of market values and their ability to spot hidden gems became the foundation for their entrepreneurial venture.

- **Blogging and Teaching:** They transitioned from simply flipping items to sharing their expertise through their blog, not only continuing their side hustle but also teaching others how to turn their thrifting hobby into a profitable venture.

Brian Winch—Founder of CleanLots: Brian's story demonstrates how a simple side hustle turned into a successful service-based business. His passion for cleanliness led him to start CleanLots, a thriving business that offers parking lot cleaning services.

- **Journey Highlights—Service Innovation:** Brian recognized the need for parking lot cleaning services and transformed it into a unique business idea. He started by cleaning parking lots himself and gradually expanded by hiring others to join his enterprise.

- **Sustainable Growth:** CleanLots experienced steady growth as Brian expanded his client base and developed a franchising model. His entrepreneurial spirit and commitment to providing excellent service contributed to his success.

Embracing Your Passions for Profit

These stories showcase how ordinary individuals transformed their passions and hobbies into profitable ventures. Whether its fashion, thrift shopping, or offering unique services, their entrepreneurial journeys began with a passion and dedication to turning their interests into income-generating opportunities.

Consider your passions, skills, or hobbies; there might be untapped potential for a side hustle that could evolve into a rewarding and profitable endeavor.

How to Get Started with a Business or Side Hustle

Let's dive deeper into each side hustle idea, exploring what's involved and how to get started. This will provide readers with more comprehensive insights into these income-generating opportunities:

Affiliate Marketing—What's Involved? Affiliate marketing involves partnering with companies or brands to promote their products or services. As an affiliate, you earn a commission for each sale made through your unique affiliate link. It requires creating engaging content, reviews, or advertisements to drive traffic and encourage conversions.

Getting Started With Affiliate Marketing:

- **Choose a Niche:** Select a niche that aligns with your interests or expertise.

- **Join Affiliate Programs:** Sign up for relevant affiliate programs on platforms like Amazon Associates, ClickBank, or ShareASale.

- **Create Content:** Develop high-quality content such as blog posts, videos, or social media posts that educate or entertain your audience while incorporating affiliate links.

- **Strategic Promotion:** Drive traffic to your content through SEO, social media marketing, email marketing, or paid advertising.

- **Dropshipping—What's Involved?** Dropshipping is an e-commerce model where you sell products without handling inventory. When a customer makes a purchase, the supplier ships the product directly to them. Your role involves marketing, customer service, and managing the online store.

Getting Started With Dropshipping

- **Choose a Niche and Platform:** Select a niche and set up an online store using platforms like Shopify, WooCommerce, or Etsy.

- **Find Reliable Suppliers:** Research and partner with trustworthy suppliers, or use dropshipping platforms like Oberlo, AliExpress, or SaleHoo.

- **List Products and Market:** Add products to your store, create compelling product descriptions, and market them through SEO, social media, and influencer collaborations.

Rental Property Income

What's Involved? Generating passive income through rental properties involves purchasing real estate properties and leasing them to tenants. It requires property management, dealing with tenants, and ensuring property maintenance.

- **Research and Financing:** Research real estate markets, secure financing, and find suitable properties.

- **Property Acquisition:** Purchase properties based on market demand, location, and potential rental income.

- **Tenant Management:** Advertise properties, screen tenants, draft lease agreements, and manage ongoing tenant relationships.

- **Property Maintenance:** Ensure regular maintenance and repairs to keep the property in good condition.

- **Stock Market Investments—What's Involved?** Investing in stocks, bonds, or mutual funds involves purchasing securities to generate returns through dividends, interest, or capital appreciation.

Getting Started With Stock Market Investment

- **Education and Research:** Learn about different investment options, risk tolerance, and market analysis.

- **Open a Brokerage Account:** Choose a reputable brokerage firm and open an investment account.

- **Diversification:** Build a diversified portfolio by investing in a variety of assets based on your risk tolerance and investment goals.

- **Continuous Monitoring and Adjustment:** Regularly monitor your investments, stay updated on market trends, and adjust your portfolio as needed.

Additional Side Hustle Ideas: Each of these ideas presents unique opportunities for individuals to generate additional income. Whether it's creating digital products, offering freelance services, or venturing into real estate, exploring different avenues can lead to new income streams and financial growth.

The way to get started is to quit talking and begin doing.
–Walt Disney

These diverse side hustle ideas are just the beginning of the vast array of opportunities available. The key is to take action, explore what aligns with your skills and interests, and embark on your entrepreneurial journey. Each path offers challenges and rewards, so take that first step towards building additional income streams.

Caution: Avoid These Mistakes!

Let's examine and expand upon the following common side hustle mistakes:

- **Investing Too Much Money:** Investing a significant amount of money upfront into a side hustle without a thorough understanding of potential returns or market viability can lead to financial strain and increased risk.

- **Avoidance Strategy:** Begin with a minimal investment to test the waters and validate the viability of your side hustle. As your business grows and proves successful, consider scaling up investments strategically.

- **Not Doing Enough Research:** Insufficient market research or a lack of understanding of your target audience's needs and preferences can lead to misguided business decisions and ineffective strategies. Be sure to do your homework by researching your niche or interest versus market needs thoroughly before you venture into it.

- **Research Strategy:** Research the market, understand competitors, and identify your target audience's pain points and preferences. Gather feedback through surveys or direct interaction to refine your offerings and improve customer satisfaction.

- **Not Charging the Right Amount for Your Services or Goods (Mistake):** Underpricing or overpricing your products or services can impact profitability and customer perception, leading to missed revenue or customer dissatisfaction.

- **Value Strategy:** Assess the value of your products or services provided and set prices accordingly rather than solely considering costs. Analyze competitor pricing to position your offerings competitively while maintaining profitability.

- **Choosing a Side Hustle You Don't Love:** Pursuing a side hustle solely for the potential income without considering personal interest or passion can lead to burnout or a lack of motivation, decrease in productivity, quality, and customer service connections as required by your clients for your business to thrive. Please be sure that you are passionate about your side hustle before you venture into it.

- **Choice Strategy:** Choose a side hustle that aligned with your interests, skills, or hobbies to maintain enthusiasm and dedication. Ensure your side hustle aligns with your long-term goals and interests to sustain motivation.

- **Giving Up Too Early (Mistake):** Abandoning a side hustle prematurely due to initial challenges or slow progress can hinder potential growth and overlook opportunities for success. Give your side hustle a chance to grow by dealing with difficulties that may arise swiftly and diligently.

- **Embracing Challenge Strategy:** Embrace challenges as learning experiences and adapt strategies rather than giving up at the first sign of difficulty. Keep the long-term vision in mind, understanding that success often requires perseverance and consistent effort. Eventually, your business will grow, take shape, and begin to serve your purpose.

By acknowledging these common pitfalls and implementing proactive strategies to avoid them, individuals can navigate their side hustle journeys more effectively. It's essential to approach side hustles with a blend of passion, prudence, research, and perseverance to maximize success and minimize setbacks.

A Story: Side Hustle Mosaic—Crafting a Secure Financial Future

RariCalamari's side businesses show financial independence and entrepreneurship. They pursued a variety of financial security-related activities to augment their income and build a secure future.

The goal was to earn more while working full-time. With their abilities, passions, and ingenuity, RariCalamari developed side companies to secure their future.

Their initial company was motivated by their love of handmade goods. They offered handmade jewelry at Etsy and craft fairs. The intricate artistry and interesting patterns kept customers loyal.

Their enthusiasm for photography led them to freelance photography. Photographing events, portraits, and landscapes lets people express themselves and generate money.

RariCalamari produced material for the digital ecosystem. Their blog and YouTube channel provide knowledge and ideas from their experience. Content that engaged readers led to sponsorships and affiliate marketing.

They examined freelance consulting, offering their expertise to small organizations needing particular help and recognizing gig economy potential. Offering insights and solutions becomes profitable and rewarding, helping companies prosper.

Their side companies modified their financial goals. Instead of quitting, RariCalamari prioritized retirement. The firms' additional money was saved and invested for a brighter future.

Running many enterprises and a full-time job needed time management and dedication. They were determined to secure their financial future.

RariCalamari's side activities diversified their income, gave them essential skills, expanded their network, and secured their financial future. Each gig was a step toward financial independence, showing that small enterprises can flourish with hard work and preparedness.

Part-Time Employment for Retirees

Here's a list of part-time job opportunities suitable for retirees, along with brief explanations of what's involved in each role:

Substitute Teacher

Requirements:

- Education Background: Typically, a bachelor's degree is required.

- Clearances: May need background checks and teaching credentials.

- Flexibility: Ability to adapt to different classroom environments.

Retail

Requirements:

- Customer Service Skills: Ability to assist customers and handle transactions.

- Product Knowledge: Familiarity with the items being sold.

- Flexibility: Willingness to work varying shifts.

Resort Worker

Requirements:

- Hospitality Skills: Providing excellent guest service.

- Physical Stamina: May involve standing for long periods.

- Adaptability: Comfortable working in a dynamic environment.

Pet Sitter

Requirements:

- Love for Animals: Caring for pets in the owner's absence.

- Reliability: Ability to stick to scheduled visits.

- Basic Animal Care Knowledge: Feeding, walking, and providing companionship.

Event Staff

Requirements:

- Versatility: Assisting in event setup, guest services, or cleanup.

- Customer Service Skills: Interacting with attendees.

- Physical Ability: Some roles may involve lifting or standing for extended periods.

Concierge

Requirements:

- Customer Service: Assisting guests, answering queries, and providing recommendations.

- Organizational Skills: Managing reservations and requests.

- Knowledge of Local Attractions: Familiarity with the area and its amenities.

Driver

Requirements:

- Valid Driver's License: Clean driving record.

- Reliability: Timely and safe transportation of passengers or goods.

- Navigation Skills: Knowledge of local routes is essential.

Tax Preparer

Requirements:

- Tax Knowledge: Understanding tax laws and regulations.

- Certification: Some positions may require certification or training.

- Attention to Detail: Accuracy in preparing and filing tax returns.

Babysitter

Requirements:

- Childcare Experience: Handling and caring for children.

- Safety Awareness: Ensuring a safe environment for children.

- Reliability: Dependable care during scheduled hours.

- Some positions may require certification or training.

Freelance Writer

Requirements:

- Writing Skills: Proficiency in written communication.

- Creativity: Generating engaging and informative content.

- Time Management: Meeting deadlines and managing assignments.

Freelance Consultant

Requirements:

- Expertise in a Field: Utilizing professional knowledge for consultation.

- Networking Skills: Building and maintaining client relationships.

- Problem-Solving: Offering solutions and guidance.

Real Estate Agent

Requirements:

- Real Estate License: Required in most cases.

- Networking and Sales Skills: Ability to market properties and negotiate deals.

- Knowledge of Market Trends: Understanding local real estate dynamics.

Librarian

Requirements:

- Love for Books: Must be passionate about books.

- Customer Service: Ability to assist customers in locating the needed or appropriate material on a timely basis.

- Ability to serve customers of various ages ranging from young kids, parents, students, and other professional adults.

- Knowledge of Specific Subjects: This may be required if working for schools or certain organizations.

- Physical Stamina: Ability to organize, lift, push, pull, sit, and stand etc.

These part-time job opportunities for retirees showcase some of the diversity of roles available but there are so many others that are not listed above such as floral arrangements, freelance photography or writing, cooking and baking special family recipes, companionship to elderly folks etc. Whether in education, customer service, caregiving, or consulting, there's a wide array of options catering to various skills and interests. Retirees can explore these roles to find a fulfilling part-time occupation that suits their preferences and allows them to contribute their expertise and experience to the workforce.

Although it is a great opportunity for retirees to provide their services and expertise, it is also recommended for retirees to work only on part-time basis. For example, it is recommended for retirees to work not more than 2-3 days (i.e., if possible, less than 8 hour shifts) per week in order for them to still fulfill their own personal retirement dreams.

If a retiree works more than the recommend hours, then they cannot be considered as "retired" as they would still be going through the daily grind of a fulltime job. Remember, that the whole purpose for you as a retiree who prefers to work a little are the following and may be even more. Please keep these in mind in order to enjoy your own retirement as well which should be your number one priority. As a retiree, you are taking on some part-time work to:

- Make extra income to substitute your retirement income.

- Avoid boredom and still be a productive and contributing senior citizen.

- Renew your own daily outlook on life by being productive.

- Make and maintain diversified connections and networks which are very important to your social and mental health.

- Support other retirees and the younger generation that needs your insights.

- Contribute your expertise and services to build your beloved communities.

- Impact your knowledge and wisdom onto the younger generation to carry out your legacies and beliefs, as well as maybe even improve on them.

- Be an advocate for things you believe in.

A Story: Rekindling Purpose—From Retirement to Enriching Academia

Retirement may seem like a long vacation from the daily grind. The beginning brought Gorf-the-Magnificent man delight and satisfaction. Boredom sets in over time.

Gorf found retirement different than expected. While quitting his 9-to-5 job was freeing, it quickly became mundane, leaving Gorf restless and purposeless.

Gorf re-discovered happiness in teaching part-time to escape this monotony. He discovered new things as an adjunct lecturer at the local university. It became a passion and great fulfillment, not simply just a job.

Gorf found safety in the classroom, where he could impact his knowledge and insight. The motivated pupils, information sharing, and intellectual debates gave Gorf energy and life. Teaching became a fulfilling, mind-stimulating career rather than a means to make money. To Gorf, teaching was like "*a paid hobby.*"

Gorf's everyday routine and the pupils' way of life were reinvigorated by his retirement from academics. The classroom became an oasis where experience and passion fostered a mutually beneficial and joyful connections.

After retirement, Gorf-the-Magnificent began a new chapter. A harmonic confluence of professional and personal satisfaction altered what it meant to be satisfied.

Exploring Side Hustles: A Step-by-Step Approach

Embarking on a side hustle journey requires thoughtful planning, self-reflection, and dedication. Here's a three-step guide to navigate through the process:

- **Create a List of Potential Side Hustles:** Start by brainstorming and jotting down part-time jobs or side hustles that align with your interests, skills, and availability. Consider various options such as freelance writing, photography, tutoring, pet sitting, driving, customer service, or retail work etc. Aim to have a diverse range of possibilities.

- **Weigh the Pros and Cons:** Once you have your list, evaluate the advantages and disadvantages of each potential side hustle. Consider factors like income potential, flexibility, required skills, time commitment, the impact on your personal health, safety, and personal enjoyment. Reflect on how each option aligns with your goals and lifestyle.

- **Develop an Action Plan:** Narrow down your choices and select the side hustle that resonates most with your skills, preferences, and circumstances. Create a detailed action plan that outlines the necessary steps to get started. This may involve setting specific goals, acquiring any needed skills or certifications, creating a schedule, and exploring initial networking or marketing strategies.

Commit to taking the first steps toward your chosen side hustle. Start by completing small tasks like registering on relevant platforms, building a portfolio, or reaching out to potential clients or employers. Consistent progress, no matter how small, is crucial to getting started.

By following this structured approach, you can effectively navigate the world of side hustles, evaluate their feasibility, and create a plan to kick-start your chosen endeavor. Remember, the key lies not just in choosing a side hustle but also in taking proactive steps to make your side hustle dreams a reality.

Transition: Make sure you are prepared to give your financial future a boost! We are going to delve into effective retirement investing methods in the next few parts. These tactics will give your money a boost, resulting in returns that you actually deserve. Join us on this very exciting voyage, and be sure not miss out!

Chapter 4: Retirement Investment Strategies

The essence of early retirement savings is encapsulated in the exponential advantages of time and compound interest. Research has shown that commencing retirement savings earlier can significantly impact the final nest egg one can amass (Business Insider, 2019). Starting to save for retirement earlier allows individuals to benefit from the power of compound interest, resulting in a more substantial retirement corpus over time.

Drawing from the principles articulated in the Business Insider article, comparing retirement savings starting at age 25 versus age 35, it becomes apparent that even a mere ten-year difference in initiating retirement savings can yield substantial disparities in the final retirement corpus (Business Insider, 2019). A graphical representation substantiates this claim, visually demonstrating the growth trajectory of retirement savings over time, portraying the divergence between the two starting ages and the resultant disparity in the final retirement balances:

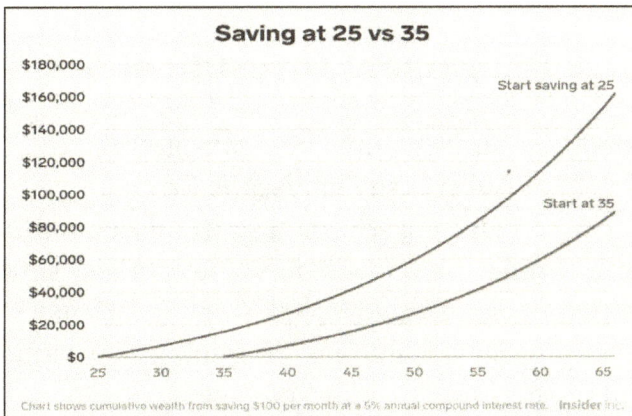

Business Insider/Andy Kiersz, 2019.

The graph itself, structured akin to the one in the aforementioned work, employs a time series plot. The x-axis delineates the years from the initial savings age to the assumed retirement age, while the y-axis signifies the accrued retirement savings balance. Two lines traverse the graph: one representing savings initiated at age 25 and the other at age 35 (Business Insider, 2019). Employing assumptions of consistent contributions, estimated returns, and compounding effects, the visual representation elucidates the significant advantage of starting earlier in the journey of retirement savings.

In concurrence with this financial wisdom, Jean Chatzky, a notable Financial Journalist, underscores the criticality of early retirement savings in her quote: *"If you're just starting out in the workforce, the very best thing you can do for yourself is to get started in your workplace retirement plan. Contribute enough to grab any matching dollars your employer is offering (aka the last free money on earth)"* (The Motley Fool, n.d.). This counsel encapsulates the essence of leveraging workplace retirement plans, especially by capitalizing on employer matching contributions, as a strategic move for those embarking on their professional journeys.

Types of Retirement Investment Accounts

Retirement planning involves navigating the ever-changing financial security landscape. In an unpredictable world, today's planning secures a safe and rich retirement. In the sea of retirement investment alternatives, simplicity often offers financial stability. A "Keep it Simple, Stupid" (KISS) approach streamlines retirement investment to focus on the best wealth-building tactics.

This lesson simplifies retirement investing with four basic retirement accounts. Each account provides professional-specific perks to boost financial security. As financial markets weave complex patterns, 401(k), Traditional, Solo, and SEP IRAs shine. Career changers' retirement planning relies on these accounts' flexibility, tax benefits, and accessibility.

We explain each retirement account's features and how they meet different career and financial objectives. Each account provides employer-matched contributions, tax-deferred growth, increasing contribution limits, and flexible investment choices to help individuals prepare for retirement.

This Guide empowers through knowledge, where a solid foundation informs decisions. The "what," "why," and "how" of retirement investing may be learned from these accounts, enhancing financial abilities for long-term success.

Throughout retirement planning, smart simplicity reflects financial success. This manual should help individuals achieve financial stability and retirement riches through simplicity. Check out each retirement investment account's benefits:

1. 401(k): The 401(k) retirement plan is a popular employer-sponsored account known for its diverse advantages:

- **Employer Contributions:** One of the most appealing aspects is employer-matched contributions. Employers often match a portion of the employee's contributions, presenting an immediate return on investment that amplifies retirement savings.

- **Tax Deferral:** Contributions are made pre-tax, reducing the individual's taxable income in the year they're made. The invested amount grows tax-deferred until withdrawal during retirement.

- **Contribution Limits:** 401(k) plans generally have higher contribution limits compared to IRAs, allowing individuals to set aside a more significant portion of their income for retirement.

- **Automatic Payroll Deductions:** The plan operates through automatic payroll deductions, fostering consistency in savings habits.

2. Traditional IRA: The Traditional Individual Retirement Account is a personal retirement account that offers several notable advantages:

- **Tax Deductible Contributions:** Contributions to a Traditional IRA are often tax-deductible, providing an immediate tax benefit. This deduction reduces the individual's taxable income in the year of contribution.

- **Tax-Deferred Growth:** Similar to a 401(k), the funds within a Traditional IRA grow tax-deferred until withdrawal during retirement, allowing investments to compound without tax implications.

- **Wide Investment Choices:** IRAs offer a broader range of investment options compared to employer-sponsored plans, providing individuals with greater control over their investment portfolios.

3. Solo 401(k) (Individual 401(k)): Tailored for self-employed individuals, the Solo 401(k) presents several advantages:

- **Higher Contribution Limits:** Solo 401(k)s allow for higher contribution limits compared to Traditional IRAs, enabling self-employed individuals to save more for retirement.

- **Employer and Employee Contributions:** Individuals can contribute as both employer and employee, maximizing their retirement savings potential.

- **Flexible Investment Options:** Similar to standard 401(k)s, Solo 401(k)s offer a diverse array of investment choices, allowing individuals to tailor their investments to suit their risk tolerance and retirement goals.

4. SEP IRA (Simplified Employee Pension IRA): The SEP-IRA caters to self-employed individuals and small businesses, with notable advantages:

- **Ease of Administration:** Setting up and administering a SEP IRA is relatively simple, involving minimal paperwork and low administrative costs.

- **Employer Contributions:** Employers can make contributions on behalf of employees, fostering employee loyalty and encouraging retirement savings.

- **Flexible Contribution Limits:** Contributions are made by the employer, with limits often tied to a percentage of compensation, providing flexibility in savings.

These retirement accounts cater to various employment scenarios, offering tax advantages, higher contribution limits, employer contributions, and diverse investment choices. Understanding the nuanced advantages of each enables individuals to select the most suitable option aligned with their retirement goals and employment circumstances.

How Does a 401(k) Plan Work? The 401(k) retirement plan stands as a cornerstone of many individuals' retirement savings strategies, offering a multitude of advantages and considerations. Here's a comprehensive breakdown addressing the core aspects of 401(k) plans:

A 401(k) plan is an employer-sponsored retirement savings account that allows employees to contribute a portion of their pre-tax salary toward retirement. Contributions are automatically deducted from paychecks and invested in various funds or investment options provided within the plan.

What Types of Employer-sponsored Plans are There? Employer-sponsored retirement plans can vary widely. Besides the 401(k), other common plans include 403(b) plans for certain non-profit organizations, 457 plans for governmental employees, and SIMPLE IRA and SEP IRA plans for small businesses and self-employed individuals.

How Is a 401(k) Different from An IRA? One primary difference lies in their sponsorship: 401(k) plans are sponsored by employers, while IRAs (Individual Retirement Accounts) are opened and sponsored by individuals. Additionally, 401(k)s usually have higher contribution limits compared to IRAs and often include employer-matching contributions.

What Is Employer Matching? Employer matching refers to the practice where employers contribute a percentage of an employee's contribution to their 401(k) plan, up to a certain limit. It's essentially *"free money"* and a key perk of many 401(k) plans, boosting overall retirement savings.

What Are the Contribution Limits? For 2022, the contribution limit for 401(k) plans stands at $20,500 for individuals under 50. Those aged 50 and above can make additional catch-up contributions of $6,500, bringing their total annual contribution limit to $27,000 (irs.gov). Please visit irs.gov for current contribution limits if you reside in the United States of America (USA) or your local tax agency if you live outside of the USA.

What Are the Withdrawal Rules? Typically, withdrawals from a 401(k) plan before age 59½ incur a 10 percent early withdrawal penalty, along with income taxes. However, certain exceptions may waive the penalty, such as for first-time home purchases, certain medical expenses, or qualified education expenses.

What Happens to Your 401(k) If You Change Jobs? Upon changing jobs, individuals have several options for their 401(k) account: leaving it with the former employer (if allowed), rolling it over into a new employer's plan (if applicable), rolling it into an IRA, or cashing out (which may result in taxes and penalties).

Understanding the intricacies of a 401(k) plan is crucial to formulating a robust retirement strategy. These accounts offer significant tax advantages, employer contributions, and investment growth potential, shaping the financial landscapes of countless individuals' retirement aspirations.

A Story: From Regret to Resilience—Trey's Journey to Financial Mastery

In the bustling city of Austin, Trey found himself standing at a crossroads. As a young professional fresh out of college, he was exhilarated to land his dream job at a local technical firm. However, the fervor of his newfound financial freedom soon collided with the remnants of past financial indiscretions.

Reflecting on his college years, Trey couldn't help but wince at the memory of frivolous spending and impulsive decisions that drained his savings faster than a Texas summer rainstorm. Credit card debts, impulsive purchases, and living beyond his means became somber echoes of his past.

Amidst the weight of regret, Trey stumbled upon a glimmer of hope—a beacon shimmering amidst the chaos of his financial missteps. The concept of "matching 401(k) contributions" echoed in his mind like a mantra of redemption—an opportunity for financial resurrection.

- **The Epiphany—Free Money in 401(k) Contributions:** Trey saw the employer's matching 401(k) contributions not just as a perk but as a lifeline—a chance to rewrite his financial narrative. "Free money," he mused, contemplating the allure of this windfall. The realization dawned upon him that every dollar he contributed was magically multiplied by his employer—a testament to the profound impact of compound growth.

- **A Pledge to Financial Redemption:** Determined to turn the tides, Trey made a solemn pledge to reclaim his financial sovereignty. He viewed each pay increase not merely as a boost in lifestyle but as a stepping stone toward financial resilience. With each salary bump, he diverted a portion to bolster his 401(k), seizing the opportunity to rewrite his financial destiny.

- **A Journey of Transformation:** The road to financial recovery was neither swift nor linear. It demanded discipline, sacrifice, and a resolute commitment to a new financial ethos. Trey's pay increases weren't earmarked for luxury; they became building blocks for a secure future—channeling into 401(k) contributions, investments, and emergency funds.

- **The Emergence of Financial Mastery:** As the years rolled by, Trey witnessed the transformation. His once-dwindling savings burgeoned into a robust nest egg—a testament to resilience and steadfast commitment. The matching contributions acted as a catalyst, accelerating his journey toward financial mastery.

Trey's story wasn't just one of redemption; it was a testament to the human spirit's resilience in the face of financial adversity. The silly financial decisions of his college years evolved into valuable lessons—lessons that reshaped his relationship with money, paving the way for a brighter and more secure financial future.

Traditional IRA: Let's delve deeper into the core aspects that define the Traditional IRA and make it a compelling retirement savings vehicle:

Tax Deferral: The cornerstone of a Traditional IRA lies in its tax-deferred growth. Contributions made to this account are made with pre-tax income, allowing the invested funds to grow without immediate tax implications. The power of compounding interest within the IRA enables the investment to grow faster than in a taxable account, as taxes on dividends, interest, and capital gains are postponed until withdrawal during retirement. This tax-deferral mechanism offers a significant advantage, allowing individuals to maximize their investments' growth potential over time.

Tax-Deductible Contributions: The Traditional IRA offers tax-deferred growth, allowing contributions to grow without immediate tax implications until withdrawal during retirement (Schwab, n.d.). This deferral strategy enables funds to accumulate more rapidly over time due to compounding interest without the burden of annual taxation (Vanguard, n.d.).

One of the significant attractions of the Traditional IRA is the opportunity for tax-deductible contributions. Contributions made to this account are often tax-deductible, meaning they lower an individual's taxable income for the year of contribution. This reduction in taxable income presents an immediate tax benefit, effectively lowering the individual's tax bill for the year. However, the deductibility of contributions is subject to certain eligibility criteria, including income limits, participation in an employer-sponsored retirement plan, and tax filing status.

No Income Limit: The Traditional IRA allows all income levels to contribute, unlike the Roth. Traditional IRAs may be formed and contributed to by high-income individuals who may not qualify for other tax-advantaged retirement arrangements. All income levels may invest for retirement with this feature.

Tax-deductible Traditional IRA contributions reduce taxable income in the year of contribution. Traditional IRA contributions may reduce taxable income and annual taxes.

Traditional IRAs are versatile retirement planning tools because of their tax benefits, including tax-deferred growth, tax deductions, and accessibility for all income levels. Its tax advantages and ability to accept contributions regardless of income let consumers save more for retirement while optimizing tax efficiency.

Solo 401(k): The Solo 401(k), also known as an Individual 401(k) or Self-Employed 401(k), is designed to help self-employed individuals or small business owners without full-time employees save for retirement. Let's take a closer look at its key features:

Tailored for Self-Employed Individuals: The Solo 401(k) functions similarly to a standard 401(k) but is specifically designed for sole proprietors, freelancers, independent contractors, and small business owners without full-time employees (excluding spouses). It provides retirement benefits that are similar to those offered to employees of larger corporations but are tailored to meet the needs of self-employed individuals.

Contribution Limits: One of the advantages of the Solo 401(k) is its high contribution potential. In 2022, self-employed individuals can contribute up to $61,000 per year. This includes both employee salary deferrals (up to $20,500, or $27,000 for those aged 50 or older) and employer profit-sharing contributions of up to 25 percent of their compensation. This generous contribution limit allows for substantial retirement savings for self-employed individuals (irs.gov).

Tax Advantages: Like other retirement plans, the Solo 401(k) offers tax advantages. Contributions made by the self-employed individual are tax-deferred, which means they can potentially reduce their taxable income for the year of contribution. Additionally, the earnings within the account grow tax-deferred until withdrawal during retirement, maximizing the potential for wealth accumulation.

Coverage for Spouses: One unique feature of the Solo 401(k) is that eligible spouses can participate in the plan, expanding the scope of retirement savings. Both spouses can contribute to the account, making it an ideal option for self-employed couples who want to maximize their retirement savings.

The Solo 401(k) is an attractive retirement savings vehicle for self-employed individuals and small business owners. It offers substantial contribution limits, tax advantages, and the flexibility to include eligible spouses in the planning process. These features make it a compelling option for those seeking robust retirement savings strategies while being self-employed.

A Story: The Wealth Builder's Voyage—Harnessing the Solo 401(k) for Financial Independence

Alex was from a modest Texas community. He was a Software Programmer but enjoyed photography. Because he enjoys capturing memories, Alex began a wedding and event photography side business.

Alex knew he had to maximize his income and secure his financial future while running his photography company. His desire for financial independence led him to the Solo 401(k). This investment provided tax breaks and huge retirement savings.

Alex investigated the Solo 401(k), excited by the prospect. This retirement vehicle for self-employed persons like him provides great financial potential.

The Solo 401(k)'s tax efficiency possibilities intrigued Alex. He might reduce his current-year tax burden by contributing photography revenues to the Solo 401(k). He anticipated enormous tax savings from the account's tax-deferred growth.

The Solo 401(k)'s $61,000 annual contribution limit motivated Alex to start saving for retirement. He could work and own, increasing wealth accumulation with big contributions.

Alex thoughtfully put part of his photography proceeds in the Solo 401(k). Tax breaks provided instant relief and financial security. His riches grew via tax-deferred gifts.

Alex considered his Solo 401(k) to be more than retirement funds. It displayed his might. This retirement vehicle saved him taxes and helped him become financially independent. He secured his financial security and freedom with the Solo 401(k), illustrating how smart retirement planning works.

SEP IRA: The Simplified Employee Pension Individual Retirement Account (SEP IRA) is a powerful retirement savings option designed for employers and self-employed individuals. Let's explore its key features in more detail:

Designed for Employers and Self-Employed Individuals: The SEP IRA is a retirement plan that caters to employers and self-employed individuals seeking a simple and flexible retirement savings option. It's designed to be easy to set up and administer, making it an attractive choice for businesses of all sizes.

Contribution Limits: One of the standout features of the SEP IRA is its generous contribution limits. Employers can contribute up to 25 percent of eligible employees' compensation or 20 percent of their net earnings for self-employed individuals. As of 2022, the maximum contribution cap is $61,000. This high contribution threshold makes it an advantageous retirement savings tool, allowing for substantial annual deposits. Please visit irs.gov for current contribution limits if you reside in the USA or your local tax agency if you are outside of the USA.

- **Income Limitations:** Unlike some retirement plans, the SEP IRA doesn't impose income restrictions for eligibility. Employers or self-employed individuals can establish a SEP IRA regardless of their income levels. This inclusivity makes it accessible to a wide range of business owners and self-employed individuals.

- **Employee Exclusions:** One attractive feature of the SEP IRA is that employers have the discretion to exclude certain employees from participation. Common exclusions include employees under the age of 21, those who haven't worked for the employer for at least three of the last five years, and those earning below a specific compensation threshold.

- **Withdrawals, Rollovers, and Distributions:** SEP IRAs follow similar rules as traditional IRAs when it comes to withdrawals, rollovers, and distributions. Early withdrawals taken before age 59½ may be subject to a 10 percent penalty unless certain exceptions apply. Minimum required distributions (MRDs) must begin by age 72 in the USA (i.e., these numbers may not be the same in other countries), and distributions are generally taxed as ordinary income.

In conclusion, the SEP IRA's flexibility, high contribution limits, absence of income restrictions, and employer discretion in employee exclusions make it a versatile retirement savings option for businesses. It offers tax-advantaged savings potential and ease of administration for employers and self-employed individuals.

Revisit Your Retirement Savings

Here's an interactive suggestion for readers to reassess their retirement savings and set a goal for additional contributions, along with a brief overview of the setting.

SMART Goals for Retirement: Now that we've explored various retirement investment options, it's time to reevaluate your retirement savings strategy. Take a moment to review your current plan and consider if it aligns with your desired retirement lifestyle.

Set a Specific, Measurable, Attainable, Relevant, and Time-Bound (SMART) Goal: Consider setting a SMART goal to enhance your retirement savings strategy.

Here is how to set SMART goals for retirement:

- **Specific:** Clearly define your retirement savings target. Instead of a vague goal like "save more for retirement," specify the exact amount you aim to contribute additionally towards your retirement accounts.

- **Measurable:** Ensure your goal is quantifiable. Determine the specific dollar amount you intend to contribute over a defined period, be it monthly, quarterly, or annually.

- **Attainable:** Set a realistic target that aligns with your financial capacity. Assess your income, expenses, and current retirement savings to ascertain a feasible contribution goal.

- **Relevant:** Ensure your goal is relevant to your overall retirement plan. Consider how this additional contribution will bolster your retirement fund and align with your retirement aspirations.

- **Time-Bound:** Establish a timeline for achieving this goal. Determine a deadline by which you aim to reach the specified contribution target.

Reassessing and refining your retirement savings goals using the SMART framework can propel you toward a more secure retirement. Take this opportunity to redefine your retirement aspirations and set actionable goals to achieve the financial future you envision.

Transition: Get ready to explore the world of Index Funds, where your money may work smarter and not just harder. In this financial trip, we'll look at the remarkable advantages and possibilities of index funds. Buckle up as we learn the keys to consistent development and financial success in the world of investment.

Chapter 5: One More Simple Investment Strategy—Index Funds

Showcasing the Long-Term Performance of S&P 500

Visualizing the S&P 500's historical performance: The S&P 500 has been a benchmark for measuring the performance of the stock market over the years. By creating a chart spanning the past 30 years (or 20, as preferred) using historical data from reliable sources like Macrotrends, you can visually illustrate the index's performance. Highlight pivotal events like the 2008 financial crisis and the 2020 pandemic to demonstrate how the market responded to major disruptions.

Highlighting Long-term Growth: Utilize the Macrotrends chart to underscore the overall upward trend of the S&P 500 over the long-term. Emphasize that despite short-term fluctuations and temporary setbacks, the market has demonstrated a consistent upward trajectory over extended periods.

According to historical data from Macrotrends, the S&P 500 index has showcased a steady upward trend over the past few decades (Macrotrends, n.d.). Investopedia highlights the significance of the S&P 500 as a benchmark for measuring market performance (Investopedia, n.d.). Utilize credible sources and ensure accuracy when referencing historical market data or providing quotes from external websites.

By visually showcasing the historical performance of the S&P 500 and emphasizing its resilience through economic challenges, readers can grasp the significance of long-term investing and understand that, despite market volatility, a disciplined and long-term investment approach has historically yielded positive results.

What is an Index Fund? An index fund is a passive investment vehicle designed to replicate the performance of a specific market index. According to Investopedia (n.d.), these funds "seek to replicate the investment returns of a designated market benchmark." Vanguard (2022) notes that index funds "provide diversified exposure to a basket of securities that mirror a market index," emphasizing their low-cost advantage and suitability for long-term investors. The Motley Fool (n.d.) highlights that index funds offer broad market exposure and low expenses, making them an attractive option for beginners or those seeking steady, long-term growth.

Investopedia describes index funds as passively managed funds that aim to mirror the performance of a particular market index. They highlight the low fees, broad diversification, and their appeal to long-term investors (Investopedia n.d.).

Vanguard highlights the core principle of index funds as mirroring the performance of a specific index and emphasizes their low-cost advantage, diversification benefits, and long-term investment suitability (Vanguard, 2022).

The Motley Fool explains index funds' approach to investing in a basket of securities that mimic a market index and underlines their low expenses, broad market exposure, and suitability for beginners or investors seeking long-term growth (The Motley Fool, n.d.).

Similarities Between Index Funds, ETFs, and Mutual Funds (Objective): All three investment vehicles share a common objective of providing diversified exposure to a range of assets or mirroring a specific index. They aim to spread risk by investing in a basket of securities. (Vanguard, 2022).

Structure: Index funds and mutual funds are managed by investment companies. Index funds are passively managed to replicate an index, while mutual funds can be actively or passively managed. In contrast, exchange traded funds (ETFs) trade on exchanges like stocks and can be bought and sold throughout the trading day (Investopedia, n.d.).

Costs: Generally, index funds and ETFs tend to have lower expense ratios compared to actively managed mutual funds due to their passive management style (The Motley Fool, n.d.).

Diversification: All three investment options offer diversification benefits by spreading investments across a range of assets, thereby reducing risk compared to investing in individual stocks or bonds (Vanguard, 2022).

In summary, while index funds, ETFs, and mutual funds share similarities in providing diversified investment options, their structures, tradability, management styles, and associated costs vary, catering to different investor preferences and strategies (Investopedia, n.d.; Vanguard, 2022; The Motley Fool, n.d.).

A brief Bio of Warren Buffett: Warren Buffett, often referred to as the Oracle of Omaha, is one of the most successful investors in history. Born in 1930 in Omaha,

Nebraska, Warren showed an early interest in investing and business. He started his journey in the investment world at a young age and gradually built up his wealth through astute investment decisions. Warren is the Chairman and CEO of Berkshire Hathaway, a multinational conglomerate known for its diverse range of investments in various industries. Renowned for his value investing approach, Warren's wisdom and long-term success have made him a revered figure in the financial world.

Warren's Preference for Index Funds: Warren's endorsement of index funds stems from several key principles he believes in, as highlighted in various sources:

- **No Need for Special Skills:** Warren emphasizes that individuals don't require exceptional skills or expertise to invest successfully in index funds. He advocates for a simple, straightforward approach to investing that doesn't necessitate extensive market knowledge.

- **Passive Investing Versus Active Investing:** Warren believes that passive investing through index funds often outperforms actively managed funds in the long run. He supports the idea that trying to beat the market through active trading or stock picking is challenging and often leads to inferior returns compared to passive strategies.

- **Emphasis on Low Fees:** Warren stresses the importance of low-cost investing. Index funds typically have lower expense ratios compared to actively managed funds, reducing fees and enhancing overall returns for investors over time.

- **Consistent Investing Through Thick and Thin:**
  Warren advocates for regular, consistent investing over
  the long-term, employing strategies like dollar-cost
  averaging. His quote emphasizes the benefit of gradual
  investment over time, suggesting that this approach
  outperforms the majority of investors who try to time
  the market (AZQuotes, n.d.).

*If you invested in a very low cost index fund—where you
don't put the money in at one time, but average in over
10 years—you'll do better than 90 percent of people who
start investing at the same time.*—Warren Buffet

In summary, Warren's advocacy for index funds revolves
around their simplicity, ability to deliver competitive
returns, lower costs, and the advantage of consistent, long-
term investment strategies. His endorsement underscores
the value of disciplined, patient investing rather than
chasing short-term gains or attempting to time the market.

Opening an Online Brokerage Account: Investing in
index funds provides a strategic path to wealth
accumulation and financial security. Whether through
traditional online brokerage accounts or innovative Robo-
advisors, individuals can easily enter the world of index
fund investing. These options not only give everyone
access to diversified investment portfolios but also provide
tools and resources tailored to their financial goals. By
exploring the steps to opening an online brokerage
account and utilizing the potential of Robo-advisors,
individuals can confidently navigate the complex
landscape of index fund investments.

Steps to Open An Account

- **Choose a Brokerage:** It is essential to research reputable online brokerages such as Fidelity or Vanguard that offer index funds. Consider factors like fees, available funds, user interface, research tools, and customer service.

- **Application Process:** Visit the brokerage's website and find the account opening section. Fill out the application form, providing personal details such as name, address, Social Security number, employment information, and financial status.

- **Fund Your Account:** Once approved, fund your account by linking it to your bank account or transferring funds directly. Some brokerages may have minimum initial deposit requirements.

Benefits of Online Brokerages

- **Diverse Investment Options:** Online brokerages offer access to a wide range of investments, including index funds, ETFs, stocks, bonds, and more.

- **User-friendly Platforms:** They provide intuitive interfaces for managing investments, conducting research, and monitoring portfolio performance.

- **Educational Resources:** Many brokerages offer educational materials, tutorials, webinars, and tools to help investors make informed decisions.

- **Customer Support:** These platforms provide access to customer service representatives for assistance and guidance regarding investment choices and account management.

- **Using a Robo-Advisor:** Robo-advisors are digital platforms that automate investment management using algorithms and computer-based models. They gather information from investors about their financial goals, risk tolerance, and time horizon to create and manage diversified portfolios.

Benefits of Robo-Advisors

- **Automation and Optimization:** Robo-advisors use algorithms to automatically create and manage portfolios, continually rebalancing them based on market changes and an investor's goals.

- **Low Costs:** Robo-advisors typically charge lower fees compared to traditional financial advisors since they require minimal human intervention.

- **Accessibility:** Many Robo-advisors have low minimum investment requirements, allowing individuals to start investing with small amounts.

- **Personalization:** Robo-advisors tailor portfolios to match individual risk tolerance, time horizon, and financial goals.

Specific Robo-Advisor Platforms

- **Betterment:** This Robo-advisor offers goal-based investing, allowing users to set specific financial goals, and creating a diversified portfolio based on these goals and risk tolerance.

- **Schwab Intelligent Portfolios:** Schwab's platform uses an automated investment methodology to build and manage portfolios consisting of ETFs, offering a range of options based on an individual's risk profile and financial objectives.

Both Betterment and Schwab Intelligent Portfolios operate as digital advisors, utilizing technology to provide personalized investment strategies without extensive financial knowledge or human advisor intervention.

Choosing an Index Fund: To understand the characteristics and benefits of prominent index funds, let's delve deeper into each of these funds:

S&P 500: The Standard & Poor's 500 (S&P 500) is a market-capitalization-weighted index consisting of 500 of the largest publicly traded companies in the United States. It is considered a benchmark for the broader U.S. stock market, offering exposure to a diversified range of large-cap companies across various sectors.

Advantages of the S&P 500

- **Diversification:** The S&P 500 provides broad exposure across sectors, reducing risk by spreading investments across a large and diverse set of companies.

- **Historical Performance:** Over the long-term, the S&P 500 has shown consistent growth and has been recommended by Warren Buffett as a reliable choice for steady growth and long-term returns.

- **Dow Jones Industrial Average (DJIA):** The Dow Jones Industrial Average (DJIA) is one of the oldest and most well-known stock market indexes. It consists of 30 large, publicly traded U.S. companies, with its movements influenced by higher-priced stocks.

Considerations for the DJIA

- **Limited Diversification:** The DJIA represents major companies but comprises only 30 stocks, which may limit diversification compared to broader indices like the S&P 500.

- **Influence of High-priced Stocks:** The price-weighted nature of the DJIA might lead to certain high-priced stocks disproportionately affecting its movements.

- **Russell 2000 Index:** The Russell 2000 Index tracks the performance of approximately 2000 small-cap companies in the U.S. stock market. These companies are generally smaller in terms of market capitalization.

Key Points:

- **Potential for Growth:** Small-cap companies often offer higher growth potential compared to larger, more established companies, but come with increased volatility and risk.

- **Higher Risk:** Small-cap stocks can be more volatile and susceptible to market fluctuations due to their smaller size and potentially limited resources.

Each index fund has unique characteristics, catering to different investment goals and risk tolerances. The S&P 500 provides broad diversification and stability; the DJIA represents established industry leaders, and the Russell 2000 offers exposure to smaller companies with potential growth opportunities but higher risk. Selecting an index fund often depends on an investor's risk appetite, investment horizon, and desired exposure to specific market segments.

Story 1: Decade of Wealth—Unveiling the S&P 500's Journey to Prosperity

In the world of investments, the S&P 500 is a testament to enduring success and wealth creation. Numerous success stories shared within investment forums and communities highlight the transformative power of consistent, long-term investment in the S&P 500 index.

Meet Jane Austin, a diligent investor driven by a desire to secure her financial future. Ten years ago, she committed to investing regular amounts in the S&P 500 index. Jane recognized the potential of this index—a collection of 500 top-performing companies that symbolize the heartbeat of the U.S. economy.

Jane's investment approach was simple yet profound. By consistently funneling a portion of her earnings into this index fund, she embraced the power of compounding and weathered market fluctuations with resilience. Regardless of market highs or lows, she stayed the course and added to her S&P 500 holdings.

Over the years, the S&P 500 mirrored the growth and resilience of the U.S. economy. Jane's diversified index fund shielded her from the risks of individual companies, ensuring a balanced exposure to various sectors and industries.

Through her diligence, Jane witnessed the remarkable transformation of her investments. What began as modest contributions evolved into a substantial portfolio, reflecting the cumulative effect of consistent, strategic investing. The compounding effect magnified her returns, propelling her wealth accumulation beyond her initial expectations.

Jane's story is one of many that demonstrate the enduring potential of the S&P 500 index. It showcases the index's resilience, ability to generate consistent returns, and role as a cornerstone in building long-term wealth.

As Jane reflects on her journey, she stands as a testament to the power of patience, discipline, and belief in the enduring strength of the market. Her story, intertwined with countless others, illustrates the profound impact of committing to the S&P 500—a journey that transformed regular investments into a formidable source of wealth and financial security.

Story 2: The Index Fund Journey—Resilience in Short-Term Setbacks

In the realm of investment experiences, some stories shed light on the challenges of building wealth through index funds. One such tale follows a journey into the world of multiple index funds, marked by initial losses, growing despair, and a temptation to sell after just two years.

Let's meet Alex Addison, an eager investor drawn to the allure of index funds and the promise of wealth creation. With enthusiasm and a desire for financial growth, Alex embarked on an investment journey, diversifying their portfolio across multiple index funds to tap into the strength of different market segments.

However, the journey did not unfold as expected during the first two years. The investment landscape was volatile and unpredictable, leading to a decline in the value of Alex's index fund portfolio. The mounting losses planted seeds of doubt and disappointment, shaking his belief in the effectiveness of index fund investments.

At a crossroads and considering selling his investments at a loss, Alex sought guidance in investment forums. Seasoned investors in these communities offered valuable advice, emphasizing the importance of long-term investing. They reminded Alex that two years is a mere blip in the grand scheme of wealth creation.

Amidst the fluctuations of the market, the investment community rallied around Alex, providing wisdom and reassurance. They stressed the significance of patience and resilience, pointing out that at 24 years old, Alex's investment journey had just begun. The short-term setbacks, though disheartening, were insignificant compared to the potential for long-term wealth creation.

This collective wisdom from experienced investors served as a beacon of hope for Alex. It highlighted the importance of weathering short-term setbacks and recognizing that index fund investments are designed to generate wealth over extended periods, surpassing the market's ups and downs.

As Alex internalizes the advice shared in the forums, a newfound determination emerges. They understand that building wealth requires patience, unwavering determination, and a commitment to a long-term vision. Within this story of setbacks over two years, the resilience to endure is poised to pave the way for eventual prosperity in the world of index fund investing.

Exploring Your Index Fund Options

Embarking on an investment journey involves navigating a vast landscape filled with opportunities and considerations. In this expansive realm, index funds offer a path to wealth creation. However, the choices within this realm can significantly impact your financial future.

Today, we embark on a journey of exploration to uncover the hidden gems among S&P 500 index funds—those that combine low costs with high returns. But our exploration doesn't stop there. We delve further, examining diverse index funds and their performance across different time horizons, from short-term volatility to long-term growth.

Join us as we navigate through data, unlock insights, and equip ourselves with the wisdom needed to make informed investment choices. Let's dive deep, comparing costs, analyzing returns, and charting a course toward financial success. Our journey begins now—a journey of exploration, enlightenment, and informed decision-making in the dynamic world of index fund investing.

Cost-Effective S&P 500 Index Funds

- **Expense Ratios and Fees:** Research various S&P 500 index funds offered by different financial institutions. Pay attention to expense ratios, which represent the annual fees as a percentage of your investment. Lower expense ratios mean fewer deductions from your investment returns over time. Compare these ratios among different funds.

- **Management Fees and Additional Costs:** Consider management fees and any other associated costs, such as transaction fees or sales loads. These costs can eat into your returns, so choosing funds with lower overall costs can significantly impact your long-term gains.

- **Fund Features:** Look beyond costs and evaluate a fund's features. Assess its tracking accuracy to the S&P 500 index, the fund's size, and its historical performance compared to the index itself. A fund's ability to closely mirror the index and its consistent performance are essential considerations.

Comparing Returns Across Time Horizons

- **Selecting Multiple Index Funds:** Expand your research beyond the S&P 500. Explore other index funds that align with your investment goals, such as international index funds, bond index funds, or sector-specific index funds. Diversification across different indexes can help mitigate risks.

- **Historical Performance Analysis:** Examine the historical returns of these funds over 5, 10, and 20-year periods. Reliable financial databases or investment platforms should be used to gather this data. Analyze returns during various market conditions, including bull markets, bear markets, and periods of economic volatility. This analysis helps gauge a fund's resilience and consistency in delivering returns.

- **Risk-Adjusted Returns:** Consider not only the raw returns but also the risk-adjusted returns. Tools like the Sharpe ratio or standard deviation provide insights into the level of risk a fund takes to generate returns. A fund may have high returns, but if it comes with significant volatility, it may not align with your risk tolerance.

- **Market Conditions:** Contextualize the returns about market conditions during the evaluated time frames. Evaluate how these funds performed during economic expansions, recessions, and periods of market turmoil to understand their behavior in different environments.

- **Consistency and Growth Patterns:** Look for consistency in returns over time and examine growth patterns. Funds that demonstrate stable, consistent growth over longer periods may be more suitable for long-term investment goals.

By conducting these analyses, you gain a comprehensive understanding of index funds, their costs, and their performance across different market conditions and time frames. This knowledge empowers you to make strategic investment decisions aligned with your financial goals and risk tolerance.

Transition: Now that we have successfully traversed the financial terrain with the help and direction of index funds, we turn our attention to the non-financial domain of retirement planning. A comprehensive examination of your health and well-being is where we're heading next.

Chapter 6: Health Is Wealth

Health is the cornerstone of wealth; an investment that yields the most valuable dividends life has to offer.—
Unknown

A decrease in health makes it more difficult to continue working, which shortens the time spent earning money and, as a result, reduces the amount saved. Health issues might cause early retirement, which means there will be less money to depend on in retirement, according to experts like The Motley Fool (n.d.).

Moreover, early retirement does not relieve all financial obligations. CNBC (n.d.) reports that ill health may increase retirement healthcare expenses. This entails the need for additional medical procedures, higher drug costs, and the potential need for long-term care. These additional costs have the potential to swiftly drain retirement resources, especially if improper accounting for them was done during the retirement planning phase.

Exercise, a healthy diet, and getting enough sleep are the three key components of good health that must be prioritized to mitigate the detrimental effects of bad health on retirement. These pillars may have a big impact on a person's retirement journey and set the stage for maintaining physical well-being.

An essential component of vitality, exercise fosters both mental and physical toughness. It does not only improves general health but may also reduce the risk of chronic diseases that might jeopardize retirement preparations.

Exercise: An Essential Investment for Longevity

Longevity requires exercise. Regular exercise boosts fitness and longevity. Several studies shows that exercise prolongs life. Exercise protects against diabetes, heart disease, and cancer. Improved cardiac function and blood circulation reduces heart attacks and strokes.

Obesity, which is related to health problems and a shorter lifespan, may be prevented by regular exercise. Exercise reduces falls and accidents in older adults by strengthening bones and muscles, lowering osteoporosis risk, and improving flexibility and balance.

Workouts improve mental and physical well-being. Regular exercise reduces melancholy and anxiety by releasing "feel-good" endorphins. Better sleep and stress management boost mental wellness.

Exercise improves your physical and mental health and helps you make friends. Group activities and sports reduce loneliness and promotes belonging by helping individuals establish new acquaintances.

Strength training twice a week and undertaking 150 minutes of moderate- or 75 minutes of vigorous-intensity aerobic exercise helps you live longer. Sustainable and engaging activities encourage long-term participation.

Although it takes exercises to live longer, exercises may improve mental and physical health and social relationships, helping us live longer and happier.

Fitness demands frequent activity, even in retirement. Exercise improves cognition. It avoids long-term ailments that might delay retirement (Mayo Clinic, 2022).

Regular exercise builds strength, flexibility, and endurance. This decreases retirement injuries and increases mobility. Active living reduces accidents and musculoskeletal disease healthcare costs (CDC, n.d.).

Workouts boost mental and physical health. It actively boosts mood, reduces stress, and prevents depression. These benefits make retirees happier and safer (Harvard Health Publishing, 2020).

Risk Reduction: Regular physical exercise has been associated with a decreased chance of developing long-term health problems, such as diabetes, heart disease, and certain cancers. By taking this preventive strategy, individuals may be able to avoid the high expenditures on medical procedures and prescription drugs throughout their retirement years (American Heart Association, 2021).

Equal importance is given to nutrition in terms of our general health. In addition to giving our bodies the nourishment they need, a balanced diet boosts immunity and encourages long, healthy lives. Moreover, it may reduce retirement healthcare costs.

Eating Right: Nourishing the Body and Promoting a Long and Healthy Life

Healthy food satisfies hunger and nourishes the body. A good diet is even more important in retirement due to its health advantages (Harvard School of Public Health, n.d.).

A diet of healthy grains, lean meats, fruits, and vegetables is essential for long-term health. This diet helps with weight loss, immunity, and chronic disease prevention.

The National Institute on Aging reported in 2023 that these advantages may lower retirement healthcare expenses:

- **Vitality and Energy Nutrition:** Healthy meals keep seniors active. A nutritious diet gives elders endurance for various activities (Johns Hopkins Medicine, 2022).

- **Balanced Diets:** According to research, balanced diets reduce high blood pressure, heart disease, and osteoporosis risk. This reduces medical costs, improves health, and prevents sickness (Academy of Nutrition and Dietetics, 2021).

Sleep

Sleep is crucial for emotional stability, cognition, and well-being, yet it is often disregarded. Sleep enhances vitality and clarity, allowing a fulfilling retirement. It is recommended that on average, adults should get between seven to eight hours of REM sleep per night. Children and elderly persons do need more, about eight to ten hours of REM sleep per night should help maintain and sustain a healthy lifestyle. Although there are several stages of sleep, the REM sleep stage is the most important stage of all. This stage is when the body and mind are completely at rest allowing the body to repair and restore itself to give you the best possible health.

- **Good Sleep for Recovery:** Quality sleep is frequently overlooked despite its health benefits. Restful sleep becomes more important for mental clarity, emotional balance, and physical health as we age (National Sleep Foundation, 2020).

The mind and memory require sleep. Retirees may focus better on hobbies, education, and socializing if they get enough sleep on daily basis.

Healthy people need sleep to recharge. Immunity, hormone balance, muscle repair, and disease resistance are a few benefits that are improved when people receive good quality sleep. (American Academy of Sleep Medicine, 2022).

Brain health needs emotional equilibrium, which sleep provides. Proper sleep reduces mood swings and stabilizes emotions. Retirees must avoid stress and worry.

Improve your health and save for retirement with objectives. Three large investments may lessen retirement planning risks due to sickness.

Tips for Incorporating Exercise into a Healthy and Pleasurable Lifestyle

A healthy and fulfilling lifestyle depends on continuing physical activity. Here are some useful and entertaining workout suggestions to help you integrate fitness into your everyday schedule:

- **Walking or Jogging:** Take a brisk stroll or jog in the neighborhood or nearby park. This is not only a fantastic method to raise your heart rate, but it also lets you take in the gorgeous surroundings and clean fresh air. Walking in the outdoors improves mental well-being in addition to physical fitness. Being in the tranquility of nature makes it a pleasant and beneficial kind of exercise by lowering stress and fostering a sense of serenity (Alberta Health Services, n.d.).

- **Running:** Running is a kind of aerobic exercise in which you move quickly while simultaneously keeping both feet off the ground. Because of all of its health advantages, it is a very popular physical exercise. Running may be done at any pace, from a stroll to an intense sprint. People of all fitness levels may benefit from this adaptable workout. It is readily accessible to anyone since it may be done on a treadmill or outside. Incorporating running into your exercise program has several benefits. It promotes weight reduction by burning calories. Frequent running helps strengthen your legs and core muscles, boost your cardiovascular health, and expand your lung capacity. Additionally, it produces endorphins, sometimes referred to as "feel-good" chemicals that lessen stress and increase feelings of well-being. Novices must begin cautiously and build up to longer and more intense runs. Wearing the right clothes and running shoes is essential to avoiding injuries and guaranteeing comfort. Stretching after a warm-up and cool-down may also help avoid strained muscles. Running is a fantastic choice whether you want to increase your level of general fitness or just get the advantages of cardiovascular exercise. It's a fun way to spend time outside and establish a connection with nature, in addition to being a terrific way to start moving. Running is a tried-and-true cardiovascular workout that allows you to choose your speed. In addition to improving your cardiovascular health and endurance, it lets you enjoy the natural beauty of the outdoors (Alberta Health Services, n.d.).

- **Group Fitness Classes (Pilates, Yoga, or Zumba etc.):** Take a look at other group fitness classes, such as Pilates, yoga, or Zumba. These classes provide chances to learn new routines and techniques from knowledgeable fitness professionals, in addition to being a fun and social way to work out.

- **Clubs or Sports Teams (Basketball, Tennis, or Soccer etc.):** Consider joining a club or sports team. Playing team sports, such as basketball, tennis, or soccer, not only keeps you in shape but also fosters friendships and team spirit among participants.

- **Interval Training:** Including interval training in your exercise regimen entails switching between quick, intensive exercise bursts and rest intervals. In addition to increasing your cardiovascular endurance, interval training helps you burn more calories in less time.

- **Stairs:** Develop the habit of using the stairs rather than the escalator or elevator. This little change to your daily schedule can make a big difference in your level of fitness and general well-being.

- **Cycling:** Investing in a bicycle and incorporating riding into your lifestyle will reward you with the benefits of great cardiovascular exercise. Explore your neighborhood, town, or city. This may also lead you to new discoveries of places that you either did not know existed or have simply forgotten about, such as a favorite restaurant or a mom-and-pop antique shop. Cycling is a fun kind of physical exercise because of its rhythmic motion, which may be both relaxing and stimulating (Cancer Research UK, n.d.).

- **Physically Demanding Activities (e.g., Swimming, Dancing, or Gardening)**: Take up physically demanding pastimes like swimming, dancing, or gardening. These activities are a great complement to a healthy lifestyle, as they increase physical fitness and also provide happiness and contentment.

Always keep in mind that finding things you really like doing is the key to sticking to a sustainable workout regimen. You can maintain your fitness and health while having fun if you do a range of workouts every day.

Variety and Progression in Gym Workouts

The diversity that comes with working out at the gym is one of its greatest benefits. You may avoid boredom by continually changing your routine and choosing from a wide variety of equipment and workout alternatives. Trying a variety of activities not only keeps your workouts interesting but also puts your body through unique difficulties. This diversity keeps your growth moving forward and helps you avoid plateaus.

Workouts in the gym also provide growth. You may progressively increase the intensity of your workouts by using heavier weights or extending the time or pace of your exercises as your strength and endurance improve. For continuous progression and to prevent physical plateaus, this gradual stress is essential.

Socializing and Motivation

Gyms also provide a social atmosphere where you may meet other fitness enthusiasts. Group workouts may inspire and build friendships. Being around productive individuals may motivate you to work harder and stay focused.

Gym workouts are great for building strength and fitness. You may have a wonderful fitness journey and achieve your goals by employing gyms' vast equipment, professional advice, variety, and social atmosphere. Thus, don't delay—start adding gym sessions to your calendar and start becoming stronger and healthier.

Gym membership offers a variety of training regimens for various fitness goals. These include group classes, aerobics, and strength training. Variety makes exercises more fun and encourages socializing (Physiotattva, n.d.).

Yoga and Tai Chi—Finding Inner Peace and Balance

Traditional yoga and tai chi boost mental, emotional, and spiritual health. Harmonizing the body and mind helps people attain balance and inner serenity.

Yoga: An ancient Indian practice, links breath and movement via postures and stretches. Stress reduction and mental clarity are achieved while strengthening, balancing, and stretching. Yoga, mindfulness, and meditation increase self-awareness.

Tai Chi: Stresses deep breathing and leisurely, flowing motions. Moving meditation is this martial art's goal. Tai chi promotes energy, flexibility, balance, and coordination while reducing stress. Tai Chi's gentle motions and awareness may calm you down.

Yoga and Tai Chi promotes body awareness and mindfulness. The objective is body-mind integration and well-being. Regular yoga or tai chi may increase health, stress, relaxation, and harmony.

Yoga and Tai Chi are excellent for the body and mind, regardless of choice. They let you escape the chaotic outer world and rest. Tai Chi's flowing motions and yoga's dynamic positions can help you achieve peace.

The advantages of these exercises goes beyond strength and flexibility. They also soothe and relieve tension. A thorough, healthy workout involves flowing motions and good breathing (Alberta Health Services, n.d.).

Dance Fitness Programs: Dancing is a great kind of exercise that goes beyond just being a social pastime. Dancing does not only increases heart rate but also brings pleasure to your exercise routine, whether you want to attend a class or just dance to your favorite music at home (Physiotattva, n.d.).

Skipping or Jumping Rope: Skipping burns calories, and enhances aerobic endurance, agility, balance, and coordination.

Jumping rope is convenient. It takes minimal gear and can be done anywhere. Only space and rope are required. Jumping rope is good for home, park, and vacation workouts.

Jumping rope regularly may improve fitness. It increases heart rate like jogging and cycling, and has similar effects. Although thirty minutes of running burns more calories than ten minutes of jumping a rope, but the effects are similar. This means that jumping a rope is more productive and time-saving.

Jumping rope helps mentally and physically. Timing hops and keeping the rope away demands skill. It may enhance hand-eye coordination and mental agility.

Jumping rope provides a good physical and mental workout. It makes being healthy, active, and fun easy. Grab a rope and jump to improve your mental and physical well-being!

Easy and Efficient Workout (Skipping Rope): This adaptable body exercise improves coordination and can be done anywhere. This adaptable, entertaining exercise is great for heart rate improvement (Cancer Research UK, n.d.).

Exercise is important, but consistency is more important than fitness. Charles Duhigg argues that major change requires exercise. Physical exercise of any kind, depending on ability and inclination, provides several health benefits. Your life improves with every action, from a brisk walk, to yoga, or housework.

The Exercise Routines of Celebrities

Typically, people who exercise, start eating better and becoming more productive at work. They smoke less and show more patience with colleagues and family. They use their credit cards less frequently and say they feel less stressed. Exercise is a keystone habit that triggers widespread change. –Charles Duhigg

Celebrities may seem to enjoy lavish lifestyles, but when it comes to fitness, they really have common habits and workout routines. Through examining their training regimens, we learn about the range of strategies they use as well as the key workouts that keep them in top physical shape. Celebrity workout regimens, whether they include strenuous sports or are ardent yoga practitioners, provide insightful perspectives on the many approaches individuals might use to attain their fitness objectives. Let's examine some well-known celebrities' exercise regimens and how these activities improve their general health and fitness.

Miley Cyrus: Embracing the Power of Yoga and Pilates

Miley Cyrus is known for her holistic approach to music, well-being, and outspokenness. Her workouts include Pilates and yoga.

Miley does yoga and Pilates on daily basis, unlike many celebrities. Miley finds comfort and security in these exercises despite her fame. Traditionally, these exercises offer many psychological and physical advantages and date back millennia.

The ancient Indian practice of yoga emphasizes breathing, meditation, and movement to build strength and flexibility. Miley candidly discusses how yoga has benefited her psychologically, spiritually, and physically. It comforts and secures her, despite her famous existence.

Miley exercises with Pilates and yoga. Joseph Pilates invented Pilates in the early 20th century to improve alignment, body control, and core strength. The low-impact workout builds muscles, improves posture, and raises body awareness.

Miley's fitness and health demonstrate her dedication to these pursuits. She publishes Pilates and yoga photographs and videos on social media to motivate her admirers to live healthy.

Miley found these behaviors reduce stress, improve mental clarity, and improve physical wellness. Yoga and Pilates' mind-body connection helps her handle celebrity demands and stay healthy.

Miley illustrates how doing yoga and Pilates daily may enhance balance and enjoyment. Her commitment to these activities encourages her followers to value their physical and emotional health and realize that well-being extends beyond appearances.

Miley enjoys yoga and Pilates, which improve mental and physical health, according to Insider (2018).

These exercises boost fitness, mental health, stress, and awareness. Miley emphasizes mind-body training for balanced fitness.

Idris Elba: The Art of Boxing

Idris Elba is versatile and dedicated. In addition to his stellar cinematic performances, boxing inspires him.

Idris had a boxing passion early on. As a youngster in East London, he experienced fighters' discipline and passion. Despite learning more about boxing in recent years, he never lost interest while performing.

With the 2017 release of his compelling docuseries "Idris Elba: Fighter," Elba debuted in boxing. The show detailed his rigorous training for his first professional bout. Idris worked hard and trained under excellent teachers.

Outside the limelight, Idris' boxing shift represented his desire to develop. Boxing pushed him psychologically and physically, showing new sides. The series inspired many by demonstrating that anyone can follow their aspirations with dedication.

Some considered Idris' boxing career a publicity hoax, but those who know him knows that he takes it seriously. Boxing helps him express himself and develop self-control, focus, and resilience.

Even as his acting career captivates audiences worldwide, Idris' boxing career shows his endless energy and determination. A great actor and inspiration, Idris bravely pursues his hobbies in acting and boxing.

Insider (2018) says that Idris' boxing regimen shows the benefits of intensive training.

Boxing improves cardiovascular health. Its intense exercises burn calories and enhance cardio. Boxing boosts stamina and endurance, improving cardiovascular health.

Boxing increases cardio, strength, speed, and agility. Boxing strengthens and coordinates various muscle groups via punches, footwork, and defense.

Boxing: Enhancing Mental Focus and Reducing Stress

Precision, discipline, and attention are needed in boxing. This activity's mental demands and devotion may reduce stress and promote mental health.

Boxing is challenging and removes tension. This sport requires complete concentration to deflect negative thoughts and daily troubles due to physical and mental hurdles. Focusing on boxing's complex methods and strategies may help practitioners unwind.

Boxing increases mental clarity, stress reduction, attention, and resilience via mental focus. Regularly doing this enhances attention, making it easier to focus and be present. Increased mental attention in many aspects of life may help with problem-solving, decision-making, and concentration.

Idris' choice to box shows how difficult yet beneficial the training is for mental, physical health, and fitness.

Chris Pratt: Variety in Fitness Routine

Actor Chris Pratt appreciates body diversity. Jurassic World and Guardians movie star Pratt exercises. He varies his exercises.

Chris exercises in several ways to stay healthy and challenge himself. He builds stamina, range of motion, and strength with aerobics, flexibility, and weightlifting.

Weightlifting dominates Chris' training. He gains muscle and gets a work-ready body. He emphasizes deadlifts and squats. He builds upper-body strength with bench and overhead presses.

Chris works out in different ways to burn calories and improve his cardio. For example, Chris does run, cycle, or perform high-intensity interval training (HIIT) exercise. He may burn fat and develop stamina with HIIT, which mixes short rest periods with intensive activity.

Chris also likes flexibility training. He does yoga and Pilates for flexibility, posture, and core strength. Mobility comes via stretching and range-of-motion exercises.

Chris' fitness philosophy promotes variety. He stays on track and develops by challenging his body with diverse exercises. Chris uses a comprehensive workout method with many activities, according to Insider (2018).

Weightlifting and resistance exercises create lean muscle, metabolism, strength, and endurance.

Cardio Workouts: Cycling, jogging, and HIIT improve heart health, endurance, and calorie burn.

Functional workouts simulate lifting, twisting, and bending. These exercises increase non-gym performance and minimize injury risk.

Chris' blend of training approaches illustrates how to develop a well-rounded fitness routine. Diverse exercises target several muscle areas, reduce training stagnation, and maintain fitness and well-being.

Kendall Jenner: Concentrated Core Workouts

Model and influencer Kendall Jenner is recognized for her fitness. Her exercise routine focuses on core training.

Kendall understands the importance of a strong core for stability, strength, and appearance. Core muscles may enhance posture, performance, and safety.

Kendall works out a variety of ways to build her core and abs. These workouts target the abs, obliques, lower back, and other core muscles. Her favorite exercises include leg lifts, planks, Russian twists, and bicycle crunches. Kendall mixes movements to work every core muscle.

Kendall maintains her core strength through attention and persistence. She does core exercises three times a week, either as part of her training or separately. She achieves her fitness goals by completing core workouts every day.

Kendall's training emphasizes core workouts. Regular commitment and a variety of concentrated exercises strengthen and tone her core, improving her health and fitness.

Kendall's focus on core exercises, especially crunches, shows the necessity of targeted training (Insider, 2018).

Improve Core Strength: Crunches, planks, and twists build abdominal muscles, improving core strength, stability, and posture.

Focus on core activities like crunches to define your muscles and tone your abdomen. These exercises isolate and train the core muscles to shape and tone the stomach, slimming the physique.

Core exercises are simple and easy to utilize since Kendall does them regularly. She might simply add crunches to her TV watching. This suggests that adding even little exercise efforts might add up over time.

Kendall emphasizes specific training for fitness objectives. Core exercises improve power, balance, and alignment, as well as appearance.

These celebrities' workouts show fitness regimes' variety and efficacy. Consistency, enjoyment, and a customized exercise regimen are stressed in every method.

Nutrition

Let food be thy medicine, thy medicine shall be thy food.
–Hippocrates

The term "nutrition" describes the food we eat and the nutrients our bodies need. It is essential to preserve one's well-being and to be in excellent health. The basic elements that our bodies need to operate effectively are found in a well-balanced diet, which consists of a range of foods from various food categories. These nutrients include carbohydrates, proteins, fats, vitamins, and minerals. Numerous health issues, such as obesity, malnutrition, and chronic illnesses, may be due to poor nutrition. To ensure that we are receiving the proper nutrients to maintain our health, we must make educated decisions about what and how much we consume.

The famous saying attributed to Hippocrates, "Let food be thy medicine; thy medicine shall be thy food," highlights the critical role that nutrition plays in maintaining our health. Building on this fundamental assertion, we will examine below what makes up a healthy diet, using data from reliable sources that support a balanced diet.

The Importance of Healthy Proteins for a Healthy Body

It's important to include a variety of protein sources in your diet to attain a well-rounded diet. Lean meats, chicken, fish, eggs, legumes, nuts, and seeds are a few examples. The amino acids needed for tissue repair, immune system support, and energy synthesis are provided by these various sources (CDC, n.d.).

It is advised to choose lean cuts of meat and poultry and to remove the skin from them. This keeps the body from consuming as many unhealthy saturated fats as possible while still giving it the high-quality proteins it needs to keep its muscles healthy and organs working properly.

Fishes High in Omega-3 Fatty Acids: Fish high in omega-3 fatty acids include trout, salmon, and mackerel. These acids are widely known for their beneficial effects on heart health because they improve general cardiovascular health, reduce inflammation, and support brain function.

Plant-based proteins are excellent sources of protein and include nuts, seeds, legumes, and tofu. They include fiber, healthy fats, vitamins, and minerals in addition to protein. You may be guaranteed a varied and well-balanced approach to nutrition that takes into account varying dietary preferences by including these items in your diet.

Fruits, Vegetables, and Legumes: The Nutritional Powerhouses

Fruits, Vegetables, and Legumes: These are very nutritious. They are brimming with essential nutrients, including fiber, antioxidants, vitamins, and minerals. Furthermore, their great variety of vivid hues symbolizes the different health-promoting substances they contain—all of which help to preserve general well-being.

Meals High in Fiber: There are several advantages to consuming a range of high-fiber plant-based meals. These meals enhance feelings of fullness, strengthen gut health, and maintain a healthy digestive system—all of which helps with weight management. Moreover, they promote long-lasting satisfaction.

Antioxidants and Phytochemicals: These are found in fruits and vegetables and it aids in the battle against dangerous free radicals. Consuming a broad variety of vibrant produce can provide you with a wealth of health benefits, including a decreased risk of chronic diseases like cancer and heart disease.

Understanding the Difference Between Healthy and Unhealthy Fats

Nuts, seeds, avocados, and olive oil all include healthy fats that are excellent for you. More specifically, these heart-healthy fats—mono- and polyunsaturated fats, for example—are essential for supporting brain function, aiding in the absorption of critical vitamins, and preserving heart health.

Limiting saturated and trans fats—which are often included in processed meals, fried foods, and baked goods—will help to improve health. However, excessive consumption of these fats may increase cholesterol and the risk of heart disease. Those who make informed dietary decisions often eat all the vital components required for their health by having a variety of nutrient-rich foods in their diet.

Salt, sodium, and potassium are needed by your body in small amounts to function properly, but consuming too much sodium can be bad for your health. While sodium has many forms, most sodium we consume are from salt which comes from processed packaged and restaurant foods. Eating too much sodium can increase your blood pressure and your risk for heart disease and stroke.

Reducing your sodium intake can help lower your blood pressure and improve the health of your heart. More than 40 percent of the sodium we eat each day comes from just 10 types of foods. Breads and rolls as the top source. Eggs and omelets are the tenth leading source of sodium. Potassium and sodium are electrolytes that help your body function normally by maintaining fluid and blood volume. However, consuming too little potassium and too much sodium can raise your blood pressure.

Most potassium we eat naturally comes from vegetables, fruit, seafood, and dairy products. On the other hand, most sodium we eat is added to packaged and restaurant foods. Foods rich in potassium are bananas, oranges, melons, cooked spinach, broccoli, potatoes, and sweet potatoes.

Potassium, Sodium, High Blood Pressure, Heart Disease, and Stroke: Increasing potassium intake can help decrease your blood pressure if you have high blood pressure. Increasing potassium intake can also reduce your risk for heart disease and stroke. Bananas, oranges, melons, cooked spinach and broccoli, and potatoes and sweet potatoes are rich in potassium (cdc.gov).

Sugars: Limiting added sugars can be beneficial and improve your health. Added sugars are sugars and syrups put in food or drinks when they are processed or prepared. Soda and packaged cookies are processed examples.

Putting sugar in tea is an example of a prepared drink. Added sugars contribute calories but no other nutritional value.

Consuming too much sugar contributes to weight gain and obesity, type 2 diabetes, high blood pressure, and tooth decay. You can reduce consuming too much sugar by not adding additional sugars to your fruits, foods, and drinks. (cdc.gov).

A Story: Rejuvenated Bites—How One Woman Found Renewal Through a Wholesome Diet

Emily Rogers was consumed by stress, fast food, and deadlines in a big metropolis. Her health deteriorated after years of juggling work and life-balance. Emily desired a change since she was fatigued, had skin issues, and fluctuated in weight.

Meal planning was difficult at first. Emily discovered that these simple diets offered her more energy after a few tries.

Emily joined a "Life-Changing Diet Changes." Forum one night for consolation. She was curious about diet and lifestyle changes and read about them.

After giving up processed foods, she began eating nutritious meals. She made colorful salads with lean meats and healthy veggies for lunch instead of ordering takeout to keep her refreshed throughout long workdays.

Fresh fruits and nuts replaced her sugary snacks. Over time, she learned to resist cakes and chocolates. Her dark skin was cleansed and sparkled.

The best change was mindful eating. Emily carefully monitored her appetite and relished every meal of her new diet. She stopped mindlessly nibbling in front of the TV and enjoyed each meal's flavors and textures.

Months passed after her unexpected diet shift. Emily's vitality was boosted, making risky jobs simple. Her reflection seemed more confident and well-groomed after years of dieting.

The greatest surprise was the nighttime calm. She slept better and felt refreshed after improving her diet. She was equally surprised that just by following her diet plan, she used less money since she cooked her own meals.

Emily demonstrated the advantages of a healthy diet daily. Physical changes affected her appearance, mood, and health.

After being fatigued and depressed, Emily became vibrant and confident. Nutritional meals restored her enthusiasm for life, not only for weight loss or skin improvement.

The Importance of Sleep for Maintaining Good Health

Getting enough good-quality sleep is essential to keeping your health and well-being at their best. Let's examine the relevance of sleep based on reliable sources to emphasize its importance.

How to Experience Less Illnesses

Getting enough sleep is essential for keeping the immune system robust. Our bodies create vital proteins known as cytokines when we sleep, which are in charge of warding off infections, lowering inflammation, and battling diseases. Lack of sleep may impair our immune system, leaving us more susceptible to common ailments like the flu and colds etc. (Health.gov, n.d.).

Restoration: A good sleep speeds up healing. Prioritizing healing gives the body more resources, accelerating recovery, and decreasing illnesses.

Good health requires a healthy weight. A balanced and nutritious diet with regular exercise will help keep your weight under control. Healthy weight demands a varied diet. Eating whole grains, fruits, vegetables, lean meats, and healthy fats are healthy and will assist you in your weight control journey.

Weight maintenance requires a healthy diet and activity. Try 150 minutes of weekly moderate-to-intense aerobics. It might be dancing, swimming, cycling, or a brisk walk. Weightlifting and resistance banding are also good for weight control.

Eating less processed food, sugary drinks, and saturated fats are also essential. The high-calorie content of such meals may cause weight gain.

Healthy weight requires a lifelong effort. You must permanently alter your diet and exercise. Weight loss should be gradual to avoid regaining it back. A healthy weight is not only for good looks, but it also enhances your health and minimizes chronic disease risks.

It takes sleep to regulate hunger and appetite. Sleep loss alters ghrelin-leptin. Ghrelin is the hunger hormone and leptin is the fullness hormone. Sleep influences hormones, increases appetite, and makes resisting unhealthy foods harder which can lead to hormonal imbalance and promote weight gain (Healthline, n.d.).

Sleep deprivation may slow your metabolism. It may impede insulin responsiveness, elevate blood sugar, increase fat storage, and elevate diabetes and obesity risks.

How to Reduce Risks of Severe Health Complications

Restoring cardiovascular health requires a regular, restorative sleep schedule. Getting enough sleep is crucial for maintaining healthy cardiovascular functioning and controlling blood pressure. On the other hand, chronic sleep deprivation is associated with an increased risk of heart disease, stroke, and other cardiovascular problems.

Sleep deprivation affects glucose metabolism and insulin sensitivity, upsetting the body's hormonal balance and contributing to metabolic diseases. This disturbance increases the risk of developing type 2 diabetes and obesity, underscoring the critical role that sufficient sleep plays in preventing metabolic diseases.

Alleviate stress and enhance mood: To lower stress and increase emotional resilience, sleep is essential. Our brains analyze emotions, reaffirm memories, and control our emotional state while we sleep.

To properly manage stress, improve our coping skills, and foster emotional stability, *we must get adequate sleep.*

Good sleep is essential for maintaining cognitive function, which includes a variety of skills, including emotional control, problem-solving, and decision-making. People may improve their concentration, attentiveness, and general mental acuity by getting a good night's sleep, which lifts their spirits and reduces stress.

The significance of making good sleep a habit and priority is highlighted by the realization of the intricate connections between sleep and general health. Beyond just making you feel relaxed, getting enough sleep is essential for reaching your highest level of physical, mental, and emotional health.

Tips for a Good Night's Sleep

Let's look more closely at several ways that sleep is vital to our health:

Keep a Regular Sleep Pattern That Includes Timing: Maintaining a regular sleep pattern helps to build the body's internal clock, which helps to regulate the sleep-wake cycle. Try to go to bed and get up at the same time every day, including on the weekends, and holidays to establish a regular schedule.

Limit Stimulants (Mentally Demanding Activities, Alcohol, and Caffeine): When it's nearly time for bed, avoid mentally demanding or vigorous activities since they may make it more difficult for you to relax and fall asleep.

Timing and moderation are key to limiting alcohol and caffeine use. Avoid or limit using these substances just before bedtime. Both can disrupt your sleep patterns and degrade the quality of your sleep. Limit your caffeine intake in the afternoon and evening, and be mindful of the impact alcohol has on your sleep.

Avoid Having a Big Dinner Just Before Bedtime (Diet and Timing): Eating large, heavy meals just before bedtime may result in indigestion and discomfort, which may make it hard to fall asleep. Give your body enough time to digest modestly. However, in cases where it's late but your body needs food, instead of a heavy meal, eat a well-balanced snack, if necessary, before going to bed. It is advised that you should not go to bed hungry.

Water and Other Fluids: Although water is good for your health, it's beneficial to drink it at least an hour before your bedtime to avoid a full bladder interrupting your good sleep. Of course, if you must drink just water just before bedtime, drink it moderately.

Turn Off All Gadgets and Engage in a Digital Fast: The blue light that electronic devices produce has the potential to interfere with the hormone melatonin, which regulates sleep. Turn off all electronic screens at least an hour before bedtime to help your mind unwind and prepare for sleep.

Perform Your Bedtime Routine: Before going to bed, the body is cued by a ritual to wind down. Brushing your teeth, washing your face, taking a warm or cool shower, or soaking yourself in a bathtub with your favorite scented soaps, and smearing your favorite lotions or oils after will start to prepare your body for a good sleep. Generally, it is recommended to go to bed clean, if possible.

Create a relaxing evening routine and engage in wind-down activities. Establish a calming bedtime routine to help your body recognize when it's time to relax. This might be as simple as dimming the lights, playing calming music, practicing gradual muscle relaxation, or practicing deep breathing techniques.

To help your body and mind prepare for sleep, try reading a book, performing some light yoga, lighting your favorite scented candle, or oil aromatherapy before bedtime.

Creating An Ideal Sleeping Environment: To create the ideal sleeping environment and to ensure that you will get a good night's sleep, make sure your bedroom is quiet, dark, and comfortably warm or cool to your body's liking. You may want to consider utilizing blackout curtains, white noise generators, or earplugs and eye covers while sleeping.

Consider Using Relaxing Methods (Awareness and Relaxing Activities): Try deep breathing exercises, guided imagery, or meditation before bedtime to unwind the body and calm the mind. According to Healthline (n.d.), these methods aid in lowering stress levels and promoting a more peaceful sleep transition.

You may significantly increase the amount and quality of your sleep by implementing these tips into your evening routine, which will enhance your overall health and wellness. As Thomas Dekker so eloquently said, *getting enough sleep is essential to maintaining our health and taking care of our bodies.*

Mental Health Matters

Exercise, Diet, and Sleep are Important for Emotional Health: A few aspects of lifestyle that have a big impact on mental health include diet, exercise, and sleep habits. Below is an in-depth analysis of these elements along with other strategies sourced from trustworthy sources:

Exercise: Exercise is vital for mental well-being in addition to being beneficial for the body. Exercise releases endorphins, which are neurotransmitters that elevate mood and reduce stress and anxiety. Regular exercise also improves sleep quality, which boosts cerebral clarity and emotional toughness.

Eating a healthy diet is essential for your mental and overall health. A balanced diet high in fruits, vegetables, whole grains, and lean meats provides essential nutrients to support mood regulation and brain function. It also raises energy levels and overall well-being.

Restful Sleep: A good night's sleep is crucial for maintaining mental and overall health. It helps to integrate memories, regulate emotions, and enhance cognitive functioning—all of which promote emotional stability and resilience.

Extra Techniques for Enhanced Mental Health

Some mindfulness practices that reduce stress and anxiety, and enhance mental clarity include deep breathing exercises, progressive muscle relaxation, and meditation. These techniques enhance mental well-being and promote calmness:

- **Establishing Goals and Objectives:** Well-defined objectives and goals provide mental fortitude and drive with a sense of purpose and direction. Breaking down highly ambitious goals into smaller, more achievable milestones reduces feelings of overwhelm and aids in maintaining concentration.

- **Show Appreciation for What You Have:** The cultivation of gratitude through acknowledging and appreciating life's benefits has a significant impact on mental well-being. Keeping a gratitude journal or just reflecting on your blessings might help you find the positive aspects of life and improve your overall wellness.

- **Focus On the Good:** Cultivating a positive attitude involves reframing from negative thoughts and stressing positive ones. Better mental health may be attained by engaging in pleasant activities, practicing self-compassion, and challenging negative self-talk.

- **Establish Relationships With People:** Social relationships have a big impact on mental health. Building and maintaining relationships with family, friends, and the community reduces feelings of isolation, increases emotional resilience, and provides support.

Combining these strategies with an all-around healthy lifestyle may help improve mental health and general well-being. Everything you do matters when it comes to promoting mental health and resilience, from practicing mindfulness to building supportive connections.

Configuring Interactive Elements

One of the best ways to maintain accountability and concentrate on your health objectives is to set and follow SMART (Specific, Measurable, Achievable, Relevant, Time-bound) goals. You may achieve your objectives by keeping an eye on your nutrition, exercise routine, and sleep patterns with the use of the following apps:

MyFitnessPal

1. **Fitness Tracking:** With MyFitnessPal (n.d.), users may log their exercises, set fitness objectives, and monitor their progress over time. Users may choose from a variety of activities and synchronize the software with fitness monitors to precisely record their physical activity.

2. **Nutrition Monitoring:** With its extensive food database, the app allows users to log meals and keep track of calories, macronutrients, and micronutrients. The app offers information on dietary patterns and allows for adjustments to meet dietary goals.

3. **Goal-setting:** MyFitnessPal users may create specific food and exercise goals. Because these goals are measurable, flexible, and customizable to fit unique needs, they support achievable health goals.

Lifesum

1. **Tailored Meal Plans:** Lifesum (n.d.) provides meal plans based on dietary preferences, health goals, and nutritional requirements. Users may monitor their food intake by selecting meals from the app's extensive database or by scanning barcodes.

2. **Water Tracking:** Lifesum (n.d.) monitors users' daily water intake and notifies them to stay hydrated throughout the day. This service ensures that users meet their water objectives for overall health, according to Lifesum (n.d.).

3. **Integration and Tracking of Progress:** Lifesum (n.d.) integrates with many fitness trackers to allow

users to sync exercise data and monitor progress in detail. This integration allows for fresh insights on food, exercise, and sleep patterns by providing a holistic view of health behaviors.

Practice Use

1. **Creating SMART Goals:** Encourage users to set SMART goals inside these apps. For instance, you might set a daily goal to walk 10,000 steps or eat five servings of vegetables by using the daily step goal function of MyFitnessPal or Lifesum's meal plans.

2. **Frequent Monitoring:** It is feasible to follow the progress in real-time by using these tools frequently. Users may adjust their fitness routines, diet plans, or sleep habits to better meet their SMART goals with the help of routine data reviews.

People may get insights about their health habits by actively utilizing these programs and implementing them into their everyday routines. This helps them make decisions and come closer to their fitness and health goals. By monitoring their progress, users may make changes for a healthy and sustainable lifestyle.

Transition: We lay the groundwork for the next act as we dissect the three pillars of health—diet, exercise, and sleep—revealing their effects on mental and overall health and revealing new tactics. Come along with us in the next chapter as we set off on a dynamic adventure through the phases of retirement, beginning with the curtain-raiser before retirement.

Empower Your Fellow Retirees

Title: Make a Difference with Your Review: Empower Your Fellow Retirees

Subtitle: Unlock the Power of Generosity

"Retirement is not an exit; it's an entrance into a world of endless connections, laughter, and the joy of writing new chapters." - Harmony Grove's center changed.

Hey there!

Retirement is a big deal, right? It's like stepping into a whole new world full of exciting adventures and possibilities. But, just like planning a big trip or solving a tricky puzzle, it takes some figuring out. That's where "Retirement Planning: One Size Does Not Fit All" comes in!

This book is like your secret weapon for navigating through all the twists and turns of retirement. It's packed with super helpful tips and tricks to make sure your retirement is everything you've ever dreamed of.

But here's the thing—I need your help to spread the word! Your review could make a huge difference for someone else who's getting ready to embark on their retirement journey.

By leaving a review, you're not just sharing your thoughts about the book—you're also helping others discover the secrets to a happy and fulfilling retirement. Imagine how awesome it would feel to know that your review helped someone else find their path to retirement bliss!

So, what do you say? Will you lend a helping hand by leaving a review for "Retirement Planning: One Size Does Not Fit All?" It only takes a minute, but it could make a world of difference for someone else.

Thank you for being a part of this journey with us. Your support means the world!

Please *click here* or scan the QR Code below to leave your review.

Warm wishes,
Skylar Waves

Chapter 7: The 5 Stages of Retirement—Stage 1

The Retirement Journey: Benefits and Difficulties

Retirement is a complex journey with many stages, each with a unique mix of benefits and difficulties. These phases provide a road map for retirees traveling through this life-changing experience by encapsulating the many emotional terrains they encounter.

The 5 Stages of Retirement

1. **Pre-retirement:** The early stage, marked by expectations and getting ready for retirement.

2. **The Honeymoon Stage:** An exhilarating, free-spirited time of discovery.

3. **Disenchantment:** Unexpected difficulties and adjustments arise when reality settles in.

4. **Reorientation and Self-Discovery:** An introspective, reorganized priorities, and purpose-driven phase.

5. **Stability:** Reaching a state of balance and accepting a contented and meaningful retirement.

Stage 1: Planning and Anticipation for Pre-Retirement

The transition is laid out in the pre-retirement period. A mixture of excitement, planning, and even fear characterize this period as people get ready to make this big life transition.

Pre-retirement Overview: In this phase, people usually plan very carefully, imagining their perfect retirement while taking care of budgetary issues and lifestyle modifications. A range of feelings might arise when one considers quitting the workforce; enthusiasm for their newfound independence, financial uncertainty, and reflection on their identity after employment.

During this phase of preparation, financial planning should be planned, retirement objectives should be envisioned, and any emotional or psychological worries around this impending change should be addressed.

We explore the subtleties of each retirement phase as we dig into it, revealing the complexities and emotional development that characterize this life-changing journey.

This sets the scene by giving a general outline of the retirement stages and highlighting the significance of the possibilities and difficulties particular to each stage, with a particular emphasis on the pre-retirement period.

Pre-Retirement Stage in Perspective

Envisioning Retirement Goals: At the beginning of pre-retirement planning, it is important to envision retirement (US Bank, n.d.). With the help of resources like the US Bank's Financial IQ, people can actively envision their retirement and match their financial plans with their goals. This approach entails more than just doing the math; it also entails creating a clear vision of the ideal retirement, which will impact future financial and lifestyle choices.

Calculating Your Needs for Money: One of the most important steps in pre-retirement is estimating retirement costs (Merrill Edge, n.d.). Considerations include healthcare, recreational activities, and unforeseen expenditures, in addition to essential living costs. People may develop a complete budget and realistic savings goals to ensure their retirement by carefully evaluating these aspects.

Planning for Housing—Reductions: A pre-retirement plan that is advised is downsizing the house, which has significant financial advantages (US Bank, n.d.; Active Super, n.d.). Assessing home requirements and considering relocation or downsizing may free up equity and reduce continuing costs, maximizing funds for retirement.

Adjustment for Retirement Age: There are significant financial ramifications to having a flexible retirement age (US Bank, n.d.). Taking into account options like working part-time or postponing retirement affects not just the sources of income but also the age at which people start taking withdrawals from their retirement accounts, which may affect their long-term financial stability.

Optimizing Input: Making the most of catch-up contributions in retirement accounts becomes an important tactic for those who are getting close to retirement (US Bank, n.d.; Merrill Edge, n.d.). By making use of catch-up provisions, they may increase their savings, making up for any shortfalls in previous contributions and fortifying their retirement fund.

Medical Emergencies: When making pre-retirement plans, healthcare planning is crucial (US Bank, n.d.; Fanews, n.d.). A thorough financial strategy for retirement security must include consideration of healthcare expenditures during retirement and research into solutions like Medicare or long-term care insurance.

Portfolio Review and Professional Guidance

To make sure that your portfolio is in line with your retirement goals, you must regularly examine it (US Bank, n.d.). To successfully navigate the intricacies of retirement planning and investing choices, seeking expert counsel at this point is essential. Having access to individualized financial counseling helps people make decisions that are well-suited to their particular situation.

These multifaceted stages of pre-retirement planning include a wide range of factors, including money, lifestyle, and health. Even if these tactics provide insightful direction, individualized financial counsel is still essential. Developing a strong and customized route to a safe and satisfying retirement requires taking into account unique situations and objectives.

Importance of Creating a Retirement Vision Board

Making a vision board for retirement is a tactical tool for bringing dreams and objectives to life (Living50, n.d.). People may make their retirement goals more concrete by envisioning them, which helps them stay motivated and clear as they prepare for retirement. By establishing explicit aims, this method helps to make retirement from an abstract idea into something more concrete and attainable.

Elements to Consider in Your Retirement Vision Board

- **Career:** Including career elements in the vision board requires thinking about involvement beyond retirement. This might include taking up hobbies, launching a small company, or volunteering. The board's visual depictions of these goals act as a continual reminder of the objectives for the future.

- **Lifestyle:** It's crucial to visualize the lifestyle you want. Showcasing them on the vision board gives a clear picture of the lifestyle one hopes to lead after retirement, whether it's traveling, adopting a better lifestyle, or taking up new activities.

- **Family:** Retirement planning often depends heavily on family goals. This might include organizing family activities, cultivating family bonds, or spending more time with loved ones. Putting objectives or pictures connected to the family on the board highlights how important these relationships are to retirement planning.

- **Property:** Retirement plans are sometimes heavily reliant on real estate selections (LinkedIn, n.d.). This might mean moving, investing in a particular property, or downsizing. These objectives are strengthened on the retirement vision board by adding images or objectives about real estate choices.

Crafting Your Retirement Vision Board

Putting together words, pictures, and symbols that symbolize retirement goals is the first step in making a retirement vision board. Photographs, magazine clippings, motivational sayings, or even hand-drawn images that capture the ideal retirement lifestyle might be included.

Getting started: People may take a few preliminary actions to start making a retirement vision board. These include considering one's own beliefs, establishing clear retirement objectives, collecting supplies for the board, and making time for creative endeavors.

As part of pre-retirement preparation, making a retirement vision board is a practical and inspiring tool. People may put their retirement objectives into a visual depiction by combining their goals for their profession, lifestyle, family, and property. This will provide them with direction and clarity as they prepare for this important stage of life.

Transition: Let's turn to Chapter 8, where we will continue to discuss the retirement stages 2–5.

Chapter 8: The 5 Stages of Retirement—Stages 2–5

A Story: Rebirth in Retirement: Susan Ballinger's Journey to Passion and Purpose

In the uplifting memoir posted on "Sassy Sister Stuff," Susan Ballinger's story of retirement serves as a lighthouse for self-discovery and rebirth. Her story develops like an engrossing book, creating a tapestry of enlightenment and personal development.

Susan set off on an unexpected journey after she retired, looking for a way to give her life fresh meaning and enthusiasm. Her experience serves as evidence that anyone can reinvent themselves at any time. She first saw retirement as an empty canvas, but she persevered and showed fortitude in navigating the unfamiliar seas.

The pivotal moment occurred when Susan ventured into uncharted territory and embraced new experiences and pastimes that ignited a passion inside her. She discovered untapped abilities and unmet goals via unexpected turns, kindling a feeling of purpose that had been dormant.

Susan's path became like a mosaic of recently discovered hobbies, from artistic endeavors to community involvement, with each step she took. Her narrative serves as a powerful example of the transformational potential of retirement—a chance to not only leave behind the known but also to go into previously unexplored areas of personal development.

Susan learned from her experience that retirement isn't only a destination; it's also a chance for reinvention and an opportunity to reach previously unrealized potential. Her story confirms the idea that retirement's wide expanse is like a blank canvas ready to be painted, one full of passion, purpose, and unrestrained satisfaction.

Stage 2: The Honeymoon Phase of Retirement

According to the source from Oak Pensions (n.d.), the honeymoon phase of retirement is an early period characterized by distinct sensations and feelings that retirees often go through. Now let's explore the aspects mentioned:

- **Non-stop Relief:** Retirees often have a profound feeling of relief at this stage (Oak Pensions, n.d.). A deep feeling of release gradually replaces the strains and anxieties of the working world. This respite may take many different forms, such as the flexibility to pursue personal hobbies and interests or the lack of regular work schedules.

- **Creation of Special Memories:** The formation of treasured memories is what defines retirement's honeymoon phase (Oak Pensions, n.d.). Retirees who have more free time and might engage in hobbies and experiences that they were unable to pursue before because of employment obligations. This stage encourages the production of memorable experiences, such as memorable trips and time spent with loved ones.

- **Increased Time for Loved Ones:** With retirement, one may spend more time with and be more available to loved ones (Oak Pensions, n.d.). Retirees may foster relationships, share experiences, and establish stronger bonds with friends and family since they have more time on their hands. Stronger relationships and more meaningful interactions are often the results of this stage.

- **Transient Characteristics:** But it's crucial to remember that retirement's honeymoon phase is just temporary (Oak Pensions, n.d.). Retirees may experience a gradual settling of their initial pleasure and feeling of freedom as they adjust to their new way of life. The retirement journey is just getting started, and it's important to understand that the early exhilaration can eventually give way to a more solid routine.

The idea of the honeymoon phase in retirement is further supported by several sources, including Physician on FIRE (n.d.) and Ambassador Partners (n.d.). They draw attention to the emotional components of this phase, emphasizing the excitement and feeling of freedom that retirees often feel when they first begin their retirement journey. These sources also highlight how feelings and experiences eventually change as retirees adapt to their new lifestyle.

Stage 3: Disenchantment in Retirement

Feelings of Disappointment and Boredom: The initial pleasure fades as retirees enter the disillusionment phase, resulting in emotions of disappointment and boredom (HealthPartners, n.d.). Retirees may feel dissatisfied if they don't have a set schedule or a sense of success in their careers. The absence of purpose and exciting activities is a common cause of this emotional slump.

Anxiety and Uncertainty: The disillusionment phase of retirement may cause restlessness and confusion, especially concerning what to do with all of this time (HealthPartners, n.d.). Retirees may feel lost in the lack of a set work schedule, uncertain about how to put their talents and energy into worthwhile pursuits.

Getting Through Disenchantment—Techniques for Overcoming Obstacles

Continue to Move and Be Active: According to HealthPartners (n.d.), physical exercise is essential for preventing restlessness and preserving mental health. Frequent exercise improves mood and fights feelings of stagnation, in addition to improving physical health.

Develop Social Networks: To prevent isolation and promote a feeling of belonging, it is essential to establish and maintain good social ties (HealthPartners, n.d.). Feelings of loneliness may be reduced by socializing, maintaining relationships with friends, and taking part in local events.

Set a Web Time Limit: Although technology may facilitate communication, spending too much time in front of a screen can lead to disengagement (HealthPartners, n.d.). Limiting internet use promotes a healthy lifestyle and keeps people from isolating themselves too much.

Always Improve Your Skills: Pursuing interests or ongoing education might support the upkeep of a sense of purpose (HealthPartners, n.d.). Discovering new hobbies or honing current abilities may rekindle a feeling of accomplishment and personal development.

Journey and Discover: Retirement is made more exciting and interesting by traveling to new locations, whether they are close by or far away (HealthPartners, n.d.). Journeys extend perspectives, provide novel encounters, and assist in severing the routine of everyday existence.

Create a Daily Schedule: Making a daily program helps people feel less aimless by giving them structure and focus (HealthPartners, n.d.). Establishing a routine helps maintain a healthy lifestyle, organize activities, and give one a sense of purpose.

Take Part in Volunteer Work: A feeling of purpose and satisfaction is fostered by volunteering and giving back to the community (HealthPartners, n.d.). Contributing to society or lending a hand to others makes one feel important and connected.

Set Priorities

Sleep and Health: It's important to look after one's physical and emotional well-being, which includes obtaining enough sleep (HealthPartners, n.d.). Making self-care a priority enhances general well-being and makes it easier for retirees to get through this transitional stage.

Further Understanding: Cornerstone Las Vegas (n.d.) and Today's Geriatric Medicine (n.d.) both discuss the difficulties associated with retirement's disillusionment phase. These sources stress the value of social interaction, regular routines, ongoing personal growth, and community service in reducing feelings of boredom and disengagement. By emphasizing comprehensive well-being and a sense of purpose, the shared techniques seek to overcome the emotional and psychological barriers that retirees often encounter at this stage of life.

Stage 4: Reorientation and Finding Yourself in Retirement

Considered the Most Challenging Stage: Retirement is frequently seen as the most difficult time for self-discovery and reorientation. Redefining identity, purpose, and personal satisfaction outside of a profession is a deep search that takes place throughout this period (Wildpine Residence, n.d.; OPRS, n.d.). Feelings of uncertainty and a quest for a new sense of self might result from the loss of a defined position that a profession formerly offered.

Reinventing Yourself: At this point, reinventing oneself becomes crucial (Retirement Tips and Tricks, n.d.). It entails pursuing new interests, pastimes, or endeavors that complement one's ideals and passions. Retirees often go out on a self-discovery quest to discover previously undiscovered facets of themselves.

Finding Your Purpose: Finding a new purpose in life takes center stage (Retirement Tips and Tricks, n.d.). Retirement catalyzes retirees to pursue pursuits of purpose and satisfaction in their post-retirement life. This quest entails reflection and investigation to match one's ideals with pursuits that give one a feeling of direction.

Strategies for Finding Passion and Purpose

To help ourselves and other retirees in our search for passion and purpose in retirement, let's examine each tactic in further detail:

1. **Try Different Activities:** Retirees may use their retirement years to experiment with a variety of hobbies. This entails moving outside their comfort zones and doing things they have never done before. Discovering new interests might come from taking pottery lessons, volunteering, gardening, or learning a new language, among other pursuits.

2. **Go Beyond Rational Thinking:** Getting involved on an intuitive and emotional level creates a road to finding genuinely meaningful activities. When pursuing new interests or pastimes, retirees might follow their gut feelings and intuition rather than only using reason. This method enables a deeper engagement with pursuits that arouse passion and enthusiasm.

3. **Self-Reflection and Questioning:** Discovering one's hidden interests requires introspection. Retirees might exercise introspection by asking themselves hard questions about *what makes them happy and enthusiastic*. It entails exploring interests, goals, and objectives to help retirees discover hobbies they may have missed.

4. **Identify Recurring Themes:** Potential interests might be identified by looking for trends or reoccurring motifs in life events. Seniors who have had moments of happiness, satisfaction, or contentment in their lives

might examine these experiences and find recurring themes that elicit these feelings. Understanding these trends might help identify pursuits or hobbies that complement innate inclinations.

5. **Take Care of Your Basic Needs:** Making physical and mental health a priority creates a strong basis for pursuing pursuits. Seniors may concentrate on pursuits that enhance health and energy, as a healthy body and mind allow for more in-depth investigation. New interests might arise from partaking in physical activities that support mental and physical well-being, such as yoga or walking, or from artistic endeavors or meditation. Grooming may also help give you a more positive outlook and lift your spirit.

6. **Tap Into Childhood Interests:** Going back to early interests or pastimes opens up a wellspring of long-forgotten passions. Rekindling excitement and uncovering hidden skills might be achieved by revisiting things that were enjoyable or fascinating during the early years. These old hobbies bring back fond memories and may inspire new ones when you're retired.

7. **Embrace Mindfulness:** Deepening awareness of one's preferences is fostered by participating completely in activities. Retirees who practice mindfulness can fully immerse themselves in events, which makes it possible to identify what offers them true pleasure and contentment. Finding activities that connect is much easier with the help of this acute awareness.

8. **Seek Inspiration:** Getting ideas from a variety of sources, such as podcasts, TED Talks, or novels, expands perspectives and piques interest. Retirees can discover new hobbies or undiscovered passions by immersing themselves in a variety of inspiring and novel viewpoints.

9. **Seek Help:** The road to self-discovery may be paved with guidance from mentors or life coaches. Seeking expert advice offers insightful advice, practical tools, and efficient methods for pursuing interests. A mentor or life coach may provide encouragement and support, facilitating the process of self-discovery.

10. **Brainstorm and Visualize:** Using visualization methods and brainstorming exercises may help make goals and wants clearer. Retirees might scribble notes, make vision boards, or draw pictures of their dream hobbies or occupations. This procedure aids in defining and securing interests or passions for more research.

11. **Seek Support from Others:** Getting friends and family involved offers a variety of viewpoints and insights about possible hobbies. Talking about hobbies with close friends and family may inspire new ideas, give new perspectives, and provide support. Their viewpoints might highlight hidden or understudied facets of possible interests.

12. **Accept Gradual Exploration:** Giving up on the fact that finding one's passion takes time releases the pressure that one puts on oneself. Retirement allows individuals to welcome the exploratory voyage and accept that their interests may develop over time.

This method promotes patience and lets natural discoveries happen without hastening the process.

Further Understanding: In a similar vein, Forbes (Pascale, 2018), Second Wind Movement (n.d.), and Insular Life (n.d.) highlight reflection, investigation, and looking for outside assistance as essential elements of finding passion and purpose in retirement. These materials advise retirees to embrace slow discovery, make use of resources, and engage in self-examination while navigating this crucial phase of retirement.

All of these tactics help retirees on their deep journey of self-discovery by providing different avenues for them to explore, find, and develop their interests.

Stage 5: Achieving Stability—Finding Contentment and a New Sense of Purpose

In this last phase, people try to achieve stability, which entails finding happiness and rediscovering their life's purpose. This stage provides the chance to build a strong foundation and feel profoundly fulfilled after overcoming several obstacles and changes. Stage five also provides a feeling of contentment and lays the groundwork for a fulfilling life by accepting the present and looking for opportunities to contribute meaningfully.

During this time, individuals look for inner serenity and harmony with their environment. They live in the present, taking each day's highs and lows with appreciation and grace. People who practice self-care and mindfulness may attain a level of satisfaction where they can appreciate the little pleasures in life.

This stage also encourages the pursuit of a fresh sense of direction. After overcoming adversity and gaining important life experience, people could find themselves desiring to make a significant contribution to society. Their goal is to leave a lasting legacy and have a good influence, whether it be through volunteering, community service, or following a passion.

Experiencing a State of Contentment and Fulfillment: Consider your accomplishments for a minute, and commemorate the important turning points in your life. Recall the effort and commitment you made to reach these objectives. You'll have a feeling of pleasure and pride after reading this perspective. To help you through the procedure, take note of these useful steps:

- **Make Time for It:** Establish a certain period each day to sit down and think without interruptions. Locate a calm and serene setting where you can concentrate on your ideas.

- **Recall Your Accomplishments:** Start by thinking about reliving your greatest successes by mentally traveling back in time. These might be tiny or large, private or business-related. Think back to times when you overcame obstacles, achieved accomplishments, and experienced development.

- **Honor the Effort:** When you think back on each accomplishment, thank yourself for all of your hard work and effort in achieving those objectives. Acknowledge the dedication, fortitude, and sacrifice that were essential to your success.

- **Embrace Your Feeling of Pride:** As you look back on each milestone, allow yourself to experience a feeling of pride and success. Acknowledge the beneficial effects your accomplishments have had on your life as well as the lives of others. Revel in the knowledge that you have reached worthwhile objectives.

- **Show Gratitude:** Give thanks for the tools, opportunities, and assistance that have helped you reach your goals. Acknowledge and express gratitude to the people or things that have contributed to your achievement.

- **Write It Down:** You may choose to journal or jot down your thoughts on a computer or a notepad. This might serve as a tangible record to review in the future, helping to consolidate your emotions and ideas.

- **Celebrate Your Successes with Family and Close Friends:** Let them know how much you've accomplished. Talking about your proud memories with others may make the environment happy and encourage others to think back on their own achievements.

You can appreciate your hard work and devotion, celebrate your accomplishments, and cultivate a feeling of satisfaction and happiness in your life by putting these doable actions into practice.

1. **Create a Calm Atmosphere:** Find a quiet, comfortable place where you may contemplate without being bothered.

2. **Create a Checklist:** To begin, make a detailed record of all the significant anniversaries and successes in your life, whether they are little victories or large ones.

Examine this list carefully, taking your time. Think back on the effort you put out, the challenges you faced, and the growth you gained from each success.

*   **Cultivate a Gratitude Practice:** Develop an attitude of thankfulness by making it a regular habit to recognize and be grateful for everything that you have in your life. Think for a minute about the positive parts of your life, relationships, experiences, and the little joys in life. Keeping a thankfulness diary where you may frequently record the things for which you are thankful may be beneficial. Now allow us to provide you with a useful and simple-to-follow guide:

    Step 1: Set aside some time each day for daily contemplation, preferably in the morning or the evening. Take some time to reflect and acknowledge the blessings in your life.

    Step 2: Give thanks for what you have: Think for a minute about all the wonderful things in your life—healthy relationships, fulfilling experiences, even the little but sometimes overlooked pleasures. Acknowledge and value the facets of your life that you may sometimes take for granted.

    Step 3—Gratitude Journal: How about keeping a dedicated gratitude diary? Spend some time each day listing three things for which you are thankful and appreciative. These might be anything from little pleasures in life to important turning points.

For example, when you have completed your education and had your first job that made money, fell in love for the first time, got married, had children, bought your first home, and got promoted at work, the laughter you shared with family and friends, your children are out of school and they are well-educated and well established, your first grandkid, the people you have met throughout your life, your relationship with God, your contributions to your community, country, and the whole world, and even the quiet and alone times that you were fortunate to have, etc.

Step 4—Mindful Reflection: Give it some thought, using all of your senses. To envision, permit yourself to feel profoundly and sincerely grateful for all the blessings in your life, and use your imagination. Focus and travel the imaginary memory lane. Let it guide you to the moments when you said *"Yes, I did it and I am a winner"*

Consistency is key; making thankfulness a daily habit is one way to achieve this. Your brain will gradually begin to concentrate on the good when you make it a habit, which will foster a feeling of pleasure and satisfaction.

Creating a Well-Balanced Routine: Create a schedule for each day that finds a harmonic way to combine your favorite activities with times for relaxation and renewal. Schedule time for hobbies, socializing, reading, or following personal interests. Make sure to provide enough time for productivity and leisure activities. To do this, kindly follow these strategic steps:

Set Your Priorities: Make a list of the things you would like to do and factor in the amount of time you typically need for each activity. You will be able to prioritize these tasks in your everyday routine with the help of this procedure.

Organize Your Time: Create a daily or weekly calendar that allows certain times for work, play, socializing, and relaxation to help you establish a regulated habit. For a healthy lifestyle, aim for a well-rounded balance.

To have a well-rounded existence, be willing to change your routine and welcome spontaneity while preserving the bare minimum of rigidity.

Setting boundaries is necessary to avoid taking on too much. *To prevent burnout, it's critical to give self-care and leisure time first priority.*

Maintaining the efficacy of your regimen requires regular evaluation. Make it a habit to evaluate how effectively your routine is serving your requirements and achieving your objectives on a frequent basis. Make changes as needed to make sure it stays in line with your interests and promotes your well-being.

Adopt a healthy way of living. Put your health first by getting enough sleep, eating a balanced diet, and exercising on a regular basis. Engage in mental health-promoting activities, such as mindfulness training, meditation, or creative endeavors. Take these easy-to-implement yet powerful steps to improve your overall health:

Include Exercise in Your Daily Routine: Make regular exercise a part of your daily routine. Choose things that you like doing to maintain long-term compliance.

Make Eating a Healthy Diet a Priority: Choose your meals carefully. For best health, choose a wide range of fruits, vegetables, whole grains, and lean protein sources.

Give Yourself Enough Sleep as a Priority: Give restful sleep the consideration it deserves. Take naps during the day if your body needs it unless this will affect your evening sleep time. Make sure you set aside enough time, roughly 7-8 hours every night to refresh your body and mind as you sleep.

Encourage Mental Health by Engaging in Mindful Practices: Incorporate mental wellness, promoting practices such as mindfulness, meditation, or relaxation methods to promote and encourage overall well-being.

Embrace Creative Endeavors: Make time for hobbies that will spark your imagination and make you very happy. Making art, writing, music, or crafts may elevate your mood and give you a great feeling of fulfillment.

Step-by-Step Guide: Engage in Reflective Journaling

Initiate a Journal: Start by keeping a notebook in which you may record different events and feelings in your life that bring you happiness, contentment, or serenity.

Capture Positive Moments: Keep track of the times that you feel happy regularly. When something wonderful happens, like a stunning sunset, a touching conversation, or a personal accomplishment, be sure to record these moments in your diary.

Think Through Difficult Times: Whenever you come into difficult circumstances, consult your diary and consider the notes you have written. You may rekindle your optimism and strengthen your sense of fulfillment by thinking back on these times.

Adopt an optimistic outlook by concentrating on the good things in your life by using your reflective notebook as a tool. Through deliberate recognition and celebration of these occasions, you may develop a positive outlook and improve your general state of well-being.

Keep Your Diary Updated on Regular Basis: Develop the practice of adding fresh, uplifting events to your notebook on a regular basis. Adopt the attitude that you should actively seek and cherish your daily experiences of happiness, contentment, and serenity.

By engaging in reflective journaling according to these guidelines, you may keep a file of happy experiences that will sustain you through trying times and bolster your feelings of satisfaction.

Make Journaling a Daily Habit: Set aside a certain period every day to journal. Take some time to reflect on and write down happy, peaceful, or fulfilling moments in your life.

Sincere Introspection: Accept sincerity and genuineness in your diary writing by expressing your actual thoughts and feelings at each moment.

Regular Assessment: Spend some time going over your diary writings on a regular basis. When confronted with challenging situations, consider these thoughts as a way to lift your spirits.

Add Thankfulness to Your Journaling: Gratitude is a discipline that you may include in your writing habit by listing the things you are thankful for each day. Incorporate self-reflection and thankfulness into your writing process.

To fully reap the rewards of enhanced self-awareness and satisfaction that come with reflective writing, make journaling a habit.

Embrace Life's Pleasures With a Renewed Purpose and Self-Identity

Embrace Your Passions: Make time on a regular basis to engage in the pursuit of your interests. Expand on the interests or activities you've developed after retiring. To make the most of your experience, join groups or organizations that share similar interests and devote yourself to them completely. Adhere to this systematic approach to successfully following your passion:

Consider, for a moment, the pursuits that have consistently captured your interest or made you happy. Make a list of the interests or hobbies you have been dying to explore more.

Schedule Dedicated Time: Set up certain times in your calendar for these pursuits. Think of them as essential obligations that put your needs first.

Make Connections with Relevant Communities: Look for local groups centered on your interests, clubs, or online discussion boards. Engaging with others who have similar interests to you may provide helpful support, inspiration, and opportunities to further your knowledge.

Broaden Your Knowledge: Make time and effort to learn more about topics that pique your interest. To build and hone your abilities, take part in seminars, sign up for training courses, or study useful materials like books and online guides.

Consistent Practice: Develop the habit of practicing and participating actively in the activities you have selected regularly. Being consistent is the key to mastering your interests and finding more fulfillment in them.

Discovering the Joy of Volunteering: Look for a variety of volunteer options that align with your beliefs and interests. Giving to various organizations or causes can give you a strong feeling of fulfillment and purpose. Make the most of your special abilities and prior knowledge to make a significant and constructive impact. Accept these calculated actions to start your journey of giving back:

Step 1: Identify issues or groups that share your interests and values:

Find Causes or Groups that Share Your Interests and beliefs by doing an extensive study. Look into non-profits or local charities that have a strong emotional connection with you.

Find the Opportunities: Make the effort to get in touch with these groups to find out about volunteer opportunities or other ways you can provide your time and expertise.

Make Baby Steps Your First Step: Start with short-term tasks or commitments to gain an understanding of what you're getting into. This will allow you to familiarize yourself with the objectives of the business and determine your place within it.

Make the Most of Your Skills: Use your gifts to change the world. Whether your forte is marketing, IT, or teaching; volunteering your abilities may make a big difference.

Think of Yourself and Be Adaptable: Assess the results of your volunteer effort regularly. Adapt your degree of participation or think about venturing into other areas in light of your own experiences.

Take Up Personal Projects that let you experiment with your interests and talents. These may include writing, art, gardening, or do-it-yourself tasks. If you put your effort into these tasks, you'll feel like you've accomplished something. This is the strategy that you ought to use:

Step 1: Look for possible project concepts: Have a brainstorming session to come up with a list of possible projects that align with your hobbies and areas of interest. Choose tasks that interest you and give you the chance to exhibit your creativity.

Step 2: Create a project plan: Create a thorough and organized project schedule. Divide it up into more manageable tasks, making sure that the deadlines and objectives are realistic.

Step 3: Make time for your project: Establish a regular time slot for project-related activities. Making progress and finishing your assignment effectively depend on keeping a regular timetable.

Step 4: Look for motivation: Get ideas from a variety of places, including books, internet guides, and trips to pertinent sites related to your project. Creativity is ignited by taking in inspiration.

Step 5: Celebrate your successes: Spend some time acknowledging and appreciating each project milestone. You'll feel more accomplished and motivated as a result of doing this.

In areas where you shine, think about providing your mentoring or tutoring skills. In addition to improving others' lives, imparting your knowledge and boosting your own sense of significance and purpose may also benefit you. You may begin mentoring by taking the following doable actions:

Step 1: Determine your areas of competence: Make a thorough inventory of all the disciplines and abilities in which you excel and are well-suited to mentor or teach others.

Step 2: Give a helpful hand: Give your time to serve as a mentor or tutor in community centers, local schools, or online. Talk to people who are eager to learn about your expertise and abilities.

Step 3: Promote experience sharing: Promote the exchange of firsthand knowledge and anecdotes that are pertinent to your area of expertise. Anecdotes from real life help to clarify concepts and establish a rapport with your audience.

Step 4: Be a proactive guide and listener: Be patient and mindful of your mentees, and make sure you actively hear what they need. Help them overcome obstacles by providing direction and encouragement while treating every circumstance with compassion.

Step 5: Monitor progress: Pay special attention to your mentees' advancement. Acknowledge and celebrate their successes and milestones, and acknowledge the influence you have had on their personal growth.

Seek out others who share your interests and establish connections with them in communities, clubs, or organizations. You may build a feeling of camaraderie, get encouragement, and have a sense of belonging by interacting with like-minded people. When looking for these links, keep the following in mind and take the appropriate actions:

Communities of Research: Join online networks, research clubs, or gatherings that share your interests. You may meet people who share your interests and interact with like-minded people by joining these communities.

Take the Initiative to Participate: Engage in active participation in the conversations, get-togethers, or activities that these organizations host. Seize the chance to impart your own experiences and learn from others.

Provide Constructive Input: To promote a feeling of community and cooperation, provide these communities with your support, direction, or viewpoints.

Encourage Connections: Establish deep ties with others who have similar interests and beliefs. Spend some time getting to know someone on a more intimate level so that you can create enduring connections that go beyond shared interests.

Participate in group projects or activities that promote teamwork to promote collaborative learning. Seize the opportunity to share your knowledge and learn from other members.

Make sure your goals and aspirations are in line with your changing interests and preferences by periodically reviewing them. Define new objectives or modify current ones as necessary. Having ongoing goals to strive for can help you remain motivated and concentrated. To actively pursue your objectives, take calculated action.

Evaluate Your Development On a Regular Basis: Set aside time at regular intervals to consider your objectives and desires. Depending on how often you want to do this, you may opt to do it quarterly, yearly, or monthly.

Evaluating your progress toward your objectives is essential. Consider how far you have come and acknowledge any accomplishments along the road. It can be essential to reevaluate your tactics and make changes in light of any unmet goals.

Adjust and Set New Objectives: Consider your hobbies and objectives now, and adjust your goals or set new ones based on your assessment. Verify that they correspond with your changing goals.

Achieving success requires setting and completing SMART objectives. Make sure your objectives are specific, measurable, achievable, relevant, and time-bound. You may ensure clarity and direction in your pursuit of these objectives by adhering to this framework.

Accountability: Discuss your objectives with a mentor or close friend to increase your level of dedication. Having someone hold you responsible encourages perseverance and commitment.

You may develop a strong sense of accomplishment, contentment, and rekindled purpose in the Stability stage of retirement by implementing these routines into your daily life. This will enrich your time with meaningful experiences and a more solidified sense of self.

Interactive Element to Help You Discover Your Purpose

Discovering your mission in life is a process of self-discovery that entails investigating many facets of your interests and life. Let's take a closer look at these activities to help you discover your purpose:

1. **Make a List of Everything You Like Doing in Life**: This activity will help you reflect on the pursuits that make you happy, fulfilled, and in the flow. Think of activities, interests, or even instances when you lose sight of time. Investigating your sense of purpose in life

might reveal important details about your interests and tendencies.

2. **Examine Your Past:** Thinking back on your life's path reveals trends, turning points, and encounters that molded you. These might be obstacles you overcome, accomplishments you're proud of, or times when you were content. Examining these examples might provide you with an understanding of what motivates you inherently and what aligns with your ideals.

3. **Get Insight from Dependable Family Members, Friends, and Expert Coaches:** Getting advice from people who are familiar with you might provide an outside perspective. They could draw attention to traits, hobbies, or abilities that you might have missed. Their insights may provide an alternative viewpoint and affirm features of oneself that correspond with possible paths toward meaningful endeavors.

4. **To Help You Process, Pose Thought-provoking, and Introspective Questions:** Asking thoughtful, introspective questions may lead to important self-discoveries. You may better define your beliefs, objectives, and long-term goals by asking yourself questions like *"What brings meaning to my life?"* and *"What impact do I want to have on the world?"* These kinds of questions stimulate reflection.

These activities are meant to be a starting point for your journey of self-discovery; nevertheless, it is crucial that you approach this process with an open mind. Accept the journey, give yourself permission to change, and realize that your purpose may have many facets and change as you mature and gain experience in life.

Recall that finding your purpose is about directing your activities and decisions toward what is really important to you rather than reaching a predetermined goal. Remain inquisitive, remain receptive to self-awareness, and acknowledge your accomplishments as you go.

Transition: The next chapter—a technical-savvy investigation—waits as we go through the transformational phases 2 through 5 of retirement planning, emphasizing the art of reinvention, purpose discovery, and passion pursuits. Come along with us as we use technology to our advantage and traverse the digital world on our way to a happy retirement.

Chapter 9: Technical Navigation in Retirement

Silver Surfers: Navigating the Tech Wave in Senior Living

Seniors have not only adjusted to the world of digital technology in today's quickly changing technological environment; rather, they have enthusiastically embraced it with amazing enthusiasm. There has been a substantial change in the way that seniors aged 65 and older interact with technology, as shown by the fact that 53 percent of them routinely use the internet (Zipdo, year not specified). Since 2013, the number of people who possess smartphones has increased by more than twofold, and an amazing 42 percent of these gadgets are currently owned by older citizens. Notably, 52 percent of senior citizens who use technology report feeling "somewhat" or "very comfortable," and 64 percent affirm that technology has had a mostly good influence on their lives (Zipdo, n.d.). This indicates that the comfort levels of senior citizens who use technology are remarkable. The significance of the role that technology plays in reshaping the experiences of older citizens throughout their golden years is shown throughout these figures. Now, let's go even further (Zipdo, n.d.):

Fifty-three percent of senior citizens aged 65 and over will have claimed that they had visited the internet regularly by the year 2021: The expanding influence of digital technology in the life of elderly citizens is reflected in their increased use of the internet. The ability to use the internet consistently may provide seniors with access to a wide range of online information, communication channels, and entertainment options, therefore improving their connectedness and involvement with the wider digital world.

Currently, 42 percent of elderly citizens possess cell phones, which is more than twice as many as in 2013: It seems that elderly citizens are becoming more comfortable with mobile technology, as seen by the huge growth in the number of people who possess smartphones. The accessibility features and different apps that are available on smartphones have the potential to improve communication, give information, and even assist activities that are relevant to health.

52 percent of elderly citizens are said to be "somewhat" or "very comfortable" with technology, and 64 percent of them feel that technology has had a mostly beneficial impact: Among older citizens, this figure demonstrates a favorable attitude toward technological advancements. There is a successful integration of digital tools into their everyday lives, with a recognition of the good effects on different areas, including communication, entertainment, and general well-being. For the majority of people, the fact that they feel comfortable with technology use suggests that they have successfully integrated these tools into their lives.

At the end of the year 2020, it is anticipated that the worldwide market for technology in senior living will reach $8.4 billion: It is clear that the senior living business recognizes the significance of incorporating technological solutions, as seen by the large financial investment in technology for senior apartments. There is a high probability that this financial commitment will be used to enhance the quality of life, safety, and healthcare services available to elderly citizens via the use of modern technology.

As reported by Leading Age, 59 percent of IT professionals working in senior care facilities utilize technology to monitor the safety of residents: One of the most important applications in senior living communities is the use of technology for the purpose of monitoring the safety of residents. It demonstrates a proactive attitude toward maintaining the well-being of older citizens by using technology solutions to improve safety and react quickly to any issues that may arise.

More than half of all elderly citizens' population use a tablet or smartphone, and four out of every five of them possess a computer: Seniors are able to adapt to a broad variety of digital devices, as seen by the widespread usage of tablets and smartphones as well as the large percentage of people who possess computers. Because of this adaptability, they are able to choose products that are tailored to their own interests and requirements, which contributes to a more individualized experience with technology.

There are 32 percent of persons over the age of 80 who use social networking sites: There is a considerable number of elderly citizens, especially those over the age of 80, who have adopted social media. This is a reflection of their desire to maintain social connections and to maintain contact with their friends and relatives. The use of social media platforms is an effective method for minimizing feelings of social isolation and preserving interpersonal connections.

An estimated 64 percent of senior citizens have a favorable attitude towards smart home technologies: The positive attitude towards smart home technologies reflects acceptance and excitement for advances that increase convenience, security, and general comfort within their living environments. The fact that this is open shows that there is a readiness to accept a home setting that is increasingly linked and automated.

More than 70 percent of senior living residences in the United States make use of some kind of electronic health record technology: The extensive use of electronic health record technology in senior living homes is indicative of a dedication to the administration of healthcare procedures in an effective manner. By streamlining the exchange of information, improving care coordination, and contributing to improved healthcare outcomes for elders, electronic health records are becoming more popular.

36 percent of older citizens feel that the use of technology may assist them in maintaining connections with their family and friends: It is important to note that the social importance that seniors place on digital technologies is highlighted by the view that technology makes interaction easier. It highlights the role that technology plays in bridging geographical boundaries and sustaining meaningful connections, both of which are essential components of general well-being yet are often overlooked.

79 percent of older citizens who have broadband internet access at home use the internet daily: The fact that seniors who have broadband internet access engage in everyday online activity is a clear indication of the significance of having a dependable internet connection. Utilization of the internet daily is indicative of participation in a wide range of online activities, including communication and enjoyment, as well as access to information and online services.

By the year 2022, one in every four senior living homes intends to have a partnership with a technology vendor: The proactive attitude that senior living communities take toward cooperating with technology providers demonstrates that they are aware of the changing environment of the electronic technology industry. This strategic relationship intends to harness the knowledge of technology providers to improve the quality of services, improve the experiences of residents, and keep up with the latest innovations in the sector.

There is a willingness to employ telehealth services among around 74 percent of the older population: Telehealth services are becoming more popular among elderly citizens, which is a reflection of the rising acceptability of remote healthcare solutions. The fact that this figure exists implies that elderly citizens are aware of the benefits that telehealth offers in terms of accessibility and convenience, which might result in better healthcare results and more proactive health management.

Approximately 91 percent of seniors require assistance in setting up and using new digital devices: Even though older citizens have a favorable attitude toward technology, the fact that they need help underscores the significance of ecosystems that are accommodating. The significance of the role that caregivers, family members, and community support play in easing the transition into the digital sphere for older citizens is highlighted by this statistic.

Electronic Health Record (*HER*) *adoption has increased by 6 percent among long-term post-acute care (LTPAC) providers since 2016:* The dedication of the healthcare industry to digital transformation is shown by the consistent growth in the deployment of EHR. The use of EHR systems in long-term care facilities improves the accuracy of data, facilitates better care coordination, and eventually leads to more effective and well-informed healthcare delivery options.

Up to 36 percent of seniors aged 65 and above play digital games: The wide variety of ways in which technology helps with leisure and cognitive stimulation is highlighted by the fact that older citizens are participating in digital games. Not only does gaming serve as a source of amusement, but it also provides an opportunity for mental engagement, which can contribute to the cognitive health and well-being of individuals today.

In 2021, only 26 percent of senior citizens were somewhat uncomfortable or very uncomfortable learning and using technologies: It is indicative of widespread acceptance and flexibility in learning new technology that the proportion of older citizens who report discomfort is quite low. Given this propensity to adopt digital technologies, it seems that there is a constant movement towards a senior population that is more aware of technology.

According to a Consumer Technology Association survey, seniors spend an average of $1,300 annually on health-related products: The substantial amount of money that is spent annually on health-related items demonstrates that elderly citizens are dedicated to making investments in their health. The awareness of the role that technology plays in promoting health and well-being is reflected in this financial investment. This includes anything from fitness equipment to health monitoring systems.

80 percent of rural homes with adults aged 60 and above have a broadband connection: The widespread availability of broadband internet access in rural communities is an indication of the efforts being made to bridge the digital divide. The availability of dependable internet in rural locations guarantees that older citizens living in these communities can enjoy the same advantages of connection, access to healthcare, and information as their counterparts living in metropolitan areas.

Within a group of 1,114 adults aged 55–100, 58 percent use smartphones, and 31 percent use tablets daily: The vast majority of people in this age group use their cell phones regularly, which is indicative of the significant role that these gadgets play in their lives. The fact that smartphones and tablets are used as daily companions highlights the multifunctionality of these gadgets, which can be used for a variety of reasons ranging from communication to entertainment to work.

In conclusion, the figures provide a convincing image of elderly citizens who are actively engaging in the digital world. Because the senior living business recognizes the critical role that technology plays, it is anticipated that the worldwide market for technology in senior living will reach $8.4 billion in the year 2020. The data demonstrates a varied integration of technology, ranging from the purchase of health-related items by seniors ($1,300 yearly) to the use of technology to ensure the safety of residents (59 percent) (Zipdo, n.d.). Senior citizens are making progress in bridging the digital gap, even though they face obstacles, such as the fact that 91 percent of them need help with new gadgets. In the age category of 55 to 100 years old, the incidence reached its zenith with the daily usage of smartphones and tablets by 58 percent and 31 percent of the population, respectively (Zipdo, n.d.).

When taken as a whole, these numbers illustrate how the landscape of technology usage among elderly citizens is always shifting. It is not just the statistics that illustrate the growing ubiquity of digital tools in their lives, but it also highlights the positive influence that these technologies have had on a variety of factors, including health, connectedness, and general well-being. These trends point to a bright future in which elderly citizens will increasingly embrace and profit from the possibilities presented by the digital age. The ongoing development of technology is pointing toward a promising future. (Zipdo, n.d.). It is a story of how invention and connection are intertwined, and it is a demonstration of the ongoing spirit of discovery that existed throughout the golden years.

Become a Tech Savvy in Your Golden Years

During the golden years of one's life, the symphony of life should be accompanied by a melody of invention and connection. In tandem with the progression of the digital era, older citizens are increasingly adopting technology, which ushers in a wave of beneficial developments. The website Aging.com asserts that technology is more than just a tool; it is also a doorway to mental and physical stimulation, a bridge to social connections, a portal through which things can be delivered to your home with ease, and a treasure trove of apps that improve regular life (Aging.com, n.d.). Becoming proficient in technology is not only a talent in this digital journey; rather, it is a kind of empowerment that paves the way for a more fulfilling and interconnected living. We are going to begin on this adventure together, during which we will investigate the enormous influence that technology may have on the golden years and discover some practical techniques to navigate the digital terrain with confidence. Let's get into further detail:

Impact of technology on seniors in a Positive Way allows me to discuss the positive effects that technology has had on older citizens:

Participating in brain-training applications or online puzzles offers mental stimulation, which improves cognitive ability and memory retention: Participating in these activities also delivers a practical benefit. Through the promotion of regular exercise routines, the improvement of mobility, and the maintenance of general health, fitness applications or virtual courses that are specifically designed for older citizens contribute to the physical well-being of adults.

Video chats with platforms such as Zoom, Skype, Teams, TeamViewer, or WebEx etc. allow for a face-to-face connection, which helps reduce feelings of loneliness: This is a practical benefit of social connection. Seniors may develop a feeling of belonging and social engagement by participating in online groups with common interests, reconnecting with old acquaintances, and sharing life updates with their families via the use of social media platforms as a means of maintaining relationships with others.

Goods delivered to your doorstep—a practical benefit: Online grocery shopping and medicine delivery services, such as Instacart or PillPack, guarantee that older citizens have access to goods without having to leave the comfort of their own homes. This is especially helpful for those who have difficulties moving about or for individuals who are going through periods when going out may be difficult.

The practical benefit of applications that improve your day-to-day life is that medication reminder apps, such as Medisafe, assist elderly citizens in managing their prescriptions and ensuring that they take the appropriate doses at the appropriate time: The use of virtual assistants, such as Google Home or Amazon's Alexa, may help with a variety of tasks, including answering questions, making reminders, and even managing smart home devices. This can significantly improve the accessibility and ease of several aspects of everyday life.

Strategies to Improve Your Computer Skills: Taking a Practical Approach to Conquering Your Fears: To improve your self-assurance, you should begin with simple activities such as writing emails or surfing the internet. Start by enrolling in online classes that are suitable for beginners or by attending local seminars that are designed to ease elders into using technology. Beginning with easier chores and working your way up to more difficult ones is an effective way to overcome anxiety.

Maintain a constructive and open mindset while taking a pragmatic approach: You should see the process of learning as a chance for your personal development. Celebrate even the smallest of your accomplishments and set reasonable goals. Put your attention on the components of technology that you find pleasurable, such as searching the internet for fascinating material or maintaining relationships with people you care about.

Reach out—a practical approach: Solicit help from members of your family, friends, or community centers in your area who are proficient in technology. Many localities provide elderly citizens with access to senior-friendly programs or tech support services. Participating in the process of learning alongside someone who has expertise may make it more pleasurable and less daunting.

Google: A Practical Approach: When you have particular questions, use Google and online tutorials to get answers. For instance, searching for "How to video call on Zoom" will reveal instructions that are broken down into steps. User-friendly lessons covering a broad variety of subjects are often available on online platforms such as YouTube. These videos cover everything from the configuration of devices to the resolution of common problems.

Take Your Time—an Approach Built on Practicality: To make learning more manageable, break it down into parts. You should devote a specified amount of time to learning a particular topic, such as the fundamentals of email or how to use a smartphone. Patience is absolutely essential, and consistent practice also helps to reinforce newly acquired abilities. Take into consideration becoming a member of senior-oriented online forums, where people discuss their educational experiences and provide advice.

In addition to this:

- **Area Agency on Aging:** Local organizations often provide face-to-face or online technology seminars that are particularly designed for older citizens. These workshops allow seniors the opportunity to get hands-on help and individualized direction.

- **Best Life Online:** This article emphasizes practical recommendations designed to improve elderly citizens' use of gadgets. These tips include knowing the settings of the device, managing passwords, and making use of the accessibility features that are built into the device.

The road toward being computer-savvy emerges as a transforming voyage as the digital curtain is unfurled, unveiling the tremendous possibilities that exist inside the domain of technology for elderly citizens. The positive impact is not merely theoretical; it is tangible in the mental acuity gained through brain-stimulating apps, the warmth felt in virtual embraces connecting loved ones across distances, the sheer convenience of goods arriving at your doorstep, and the seamless integration of applications that elevate the cadence of daily life. A number of these benefits are tangible. A compass for navigating the digital landscape is formed by the advice that is supplied, which ranges from overcoming phobias to gradually embracing Google and the encouragement to take one's time (Aging.com, n.d.). The feeling is further echoed by AAAWM (n.d.) and Best Life Online (n.d.), both of which provide an understanding of how to overcome technological obstacles and become proficient with various gadgets (AAAWM, n.d.) (Best Life Online, n.d.). During the golden years of life, technology is not only a feature; rather, it is a bright thread that weaves a narrative of empowerment, connection, and continuous learning. This is because the path of life is a tough one. Let us thus immerse ourselves in this digital symphony, where every click and touch reverberates with the melody of a life that is abundantly linked.

Through the implementation of these useful suggestions and the use of accessible information, you will be able to confidently embrace technology to enhance your life in a variety of ways, including maintaining social connections and effectively managing everyday duties. One of the most important things to do is to take baby steps, to look for assistance when you feel you need it, and to recognize the practical advantages that technology provides to your everyday activities.

A Story: Silver Surfers Unleashed—A Digital Encore in the Golden Years

In serene Harmony Grove, a group of retirees at Golden Meadows Retirement Community found they were about to start a new chapter in their lives. Amid lush lawns and charming cottages, this group, which had amassed many memories over decades, was ready to go on an adventure that would change their senior years.

Everything began when Evelyn, a lively retiree with a contagious love for life, discovered social media. She introduced her neighbors to Facebook, Instagram, and video chats. She did this with sparkling eyes. A simple instruction became a revelation.

Golden Meadows quickly became a popular online social hub. The social internet let retired people reconnect with far-flung friends and family. Their laughter filled the virtual corridors of their new digital realm, and their faces lit up as they recalled their shared adventures.

Residents may dance to their favorite music in the community's cozy common space during virtual dance parties. Every video exchange showed the resilience of friendship, showing that memories and seeing familiar faces could overcome physical distance.

But the story continued. To enrich their experiences, the retirees, now called "Silver Surfers," found new friends who enjoyed gardening, reading, and online cooking classes via internet discussion forums and interest groups. The retirement community became a vibrant melting pot with many interests, and each day provided new opportunities to connect and discover common ground.

After surfing the digital waves, the Silver Surfers discovered retirement was only the start of a new adventure. Their internet journeys showcased the power of human connection and the endless spirit of discovery. Each click and video communication laid the basis for a legacy of friendship and community that would extend beyond their peaceful retirement hideaway.

Golden Meadows Retirement Community proved that "Retirement is not an exit; it's an entrance into a world of endless connections, laughter, and the joy of writing new chapters, one video call at a time." Harmony Grove's center changed.

Navigating Technology Safely for Seniors

The world of technology is always shifting, and as a result, elderly citizens are finding themselves on a voyage of discovery, trying to unleash the possibilities of technological connectivity and knowledge. Certain guideposts become important as they begin on this digital voyage to guarantee that they will have an experience that is both secure and enriching. While you are on the internet surfing and participating in your favorite activities, *please be careful.* Even though the internet is a beautiful place to get things done, it also includes untrustworthy persons whose sole goals are to take advantage of not just elderly persons but to anyone who is vulnerable including children and adults alike. They impersonate your family and friends to trick you into giving them your personal information which they will in turn use against you in the most unique ways. Scammers are very hard to spot even for people who are tech savvy.

Caution: *Extreme care must be taken while communicating via the internet. Remember, any time an activity does not make sense, someone wants to take over your smart device online, or calls you to give them information, **do not oblige**. Shut down your smart gadget and seek help in-person from a known source such as you family member etc. Remember that you have the power to stop scammers but if you don't, they will steal from you and your family or worse.*

Below are some safety measures that you can take to stop scammers:

1. **Strong Passwords:** In the realm of the internet, a strong fortress is constructed upon the foundation of strong passwords. According to Senior Resource Connectors (n.d.), the creation of passwords that are a mix of letters, numbers, and symbols serves as a powerful defense mechanism against unwanted access. Imagine that your password plays the role of a guardian of a holy vault, guaranteeing that only those who are trustworthy may enter. This will ensure that your digital identity is as safe as the walls of a medieval fortress.

   It is strongly recommended that seniors should NEVER share their passwords with others unknown to them. It is also safer to change the password from time-to-time. If possible, avoid writing down passwords. If you have to write it down, ensure that it is well concealed from others.

2. **Protecting Your Data:** The protection of your data is essential since your digital identity is a priceless tapestry that is weaved with personal information. To shield this tapestry from harm, a watchful guard is required. Senior Services of America is one of the organizations that advocates for the use of firewalls, antivirus software, and the routine upgrading of equipment to strengthen defenses against cyber-attacks (Senior Services of America, n.d.). Taking care of your digital area is like caring for a garden; it guarantees that you have a thriving environment that is free from potentially unwanted visitors.

3. **Be Wary of Con Artists:** In the enormous area of the internet, there are digital con artists who are willing to take advantage of trust. Senior citizens must empower themselves with information and acquire the ability to identify phishing attempts and fraudulent schemes. According to Senior Resource Connectors (n.d.), individuals may protect themselves from falling victim to these online predators by maintaining vigilance and doubting the legitimacy of unwanted communications or emails.

4. **Everyone Requires Assistance Occasionally:** Even the most experienced explorers need the assistance of guides. Finding one's way through the digital world is not an exception. Seniors are urged to seek assistance from friends, family members, or members of the community who are knowledgeable in technology. This is in recognition of the fact that

everyone needs support at some point in their lives. This spirit of collaboration assures that a communal journey will be undertaken, during which knowledge will be exchanged and obstacles will be confronted jointly.

5. **Explore online resources:** The internet sphere is a vast cosmos that is brimming with riches that are just waiting to be discovered. Explore the resources that are available online. Seniors are strongly encouraged to investigate the enormous variety of materials that are available online. A treasure mine of information and pleasure may be found in these sites, which range from instructional platforms to entertainment hotspots. According to Verve Senior Living (n.d.), navigating this digital universe transforms into an exciting experience that makes it possible to access new worlds of knowledge and connection.

As seniors embark on this digital journey, they transform into intrepid navigators by equipping themselves with robust passwords, strengthened data security, a sharp eye for fraud, a willingness to seek assistance, and an excitement to explore. To ensure that the senior population can navigate securely through the waves of technology and take advantage of the many chances that are yet to come, the digital horizon has an infinite number of options for connection, study, and pleasure.

Transition: Weaving a colorful tapestry of social connections is our next stop as we tear down the barriers of fear and promote an acceptance of technology in this chapter, paving the way for a safer digital voyage. In the next chapter, we will examine the craft of creating and preserving significant social networks in the digital era.

Chapter 10: Building and Nurturing Social Networks in Retirement

Human beings are social creatures. We are social not just in the trivial sense that we like company, and not just in the obvious sense that we each depend on others. We are social in a more elemental way: simply to exist as a normal human being requires interaction with other people.–Atul Gawande

Why Social Connection Benefits Our Health and Happiness

Social ties play a vital role in the health and happiness of seniors by weaving a story of great significance into the fabric of their lives. These strands, which are examined in The Legacy of Farmington, start with the essential idea of belonging and build a strong sense of community. This bond does more than just foster friendship; it coordinates an active lifestyle, a dance that maintains the body and mind in harmony. The rhythm of laughter in these social gatherings creates a calming atmosphere by acting as a potent stress reliever. These social ties serve as a strong barrier against mental health issues, a source of increased enjoyment, and a source of intellectual stimulation as life's symphony develops. Consistent with these observations, findings from Forbes and the Greater Good Science Center at Berkeley complement each other, providing more viewpoints on the critical function that social networks play in preserving the health of the elderly (Greater Good Science Center, n.d. and Forbes, n.d.):

1. **A Strong Feeling of Belonging:** Social interaction is essential to helping seniors develop a strong feeling

of belonging, which is a vital component that greatly improves their general well-being. To do this, take into consideration the detailed instructions below:

2. **Determine Personal Interests:** Assist elders in determining and pursuing their interests. Finding something in common with people—be it a shared pastime, interest, or passion—forms the cornerstone of lasting interactions.

3. **Attend Local Community Events:** Being involved in the community offers you the chance to network with others who share your interests. This might include going to classes, joining groups, or attending social events hosted by the neighborhood.

4. **Volunteer or Join a Group:** Seniors may make connections with others who share their values and views by volunteering for a cause they are passionate about or by joining a group focused on a common interest. This common goal encourages a more profound feeling of inclusion.

5. **Attend Social Events:** Participating in community events, such as potlucks, coffee shops, or game evenings, regularly fosters informal contacts. These environments encourage the development of relationships based on common experiences.

6. **Make use of Technology for Connection:** Make use of technology to maintain relationships with loved ones. When face-to-face interaction may be difficult, video chats, social media, or online discussion boards provide ways to keep connections going.

7. **Engage in Senior Center or Program Activities:** Senior centers and programs provide activities specifically designed for senior citizens. To build a sense of community, seniors should be encouraged to take part in these events and connect with peers who have similar interests and lifestyles.

8. **Show Friendliness and Openness:** When elders encounter new individuals, encourage them to show friendliness and openness. A welcoming environment that is favorable to forming relationships is created by a genuine smile and a desire to participate in talks.

9. **Tell Your Own Story:** Telling your own story and experiences might help others overcome hurdles. People get to know one another better as a result of this vulnerability, which builds genuine connections based on similar experiences and life stories.

By taking these simple actions, seniors may actively foster a sense of community and build a network of support that not only increases their emotional stability but also gives them a sense of purpose.

Maintaining Activity

Seniors who regularly engage in social interactions are more likely to be physically active, which is beneficial to their general health and well-being. Here's how to combine social interaction with physical activity, step-by-step:

1. **Identify Preferred Activities:** To begin, decide which physical pursuits meet your tastes and degree of fitness. Choosing pleasurable hobbies enhances the

chance of persistent involvement, whether the activity is gardening, dancing, or walking.

2. **Join in Group Fitness Programs:** Seniors may enjoy a controlled and encouraging atmosphere by taking part in group fitness programs at their neighborhood gym or community center. Encouraging relationships among members of the group provides a feeling of responsibility and drive.

3. **Explore Outdoor Activities:** Plan or attend outdoor activities with friends or neighborhood associations. In addition to providing physical advantages, outdoor activities such as picnics, group cycling, and nature hikes also provide a casual and comfortable environment for socialization.

4. **Play Team Sports:** If you're a fan of team sports, signing up for neighborhood leagues or recreational teams may be a fun way to be active. The dynamics of the team foster a feeling of community and regular engagement.

5. **Socializing and Physical Activities Together:** Incorporate socializing into physical activities. For example, seniors might benefit from social interaction and physical activity at the same time by starting walking clubs or attending community fitness programs.

6. **Use Technology for Fitness Challenges:** Join friends and family in virtual fitness challenges by embracing technology. Step challenges and virtual training sessions are just two examples of how

technology can be an engaging and enjoyable method to keep active and spend time with loved ones.

7. **Take Wellness Programs:** Senior-focused wellness programs encompassing a variety of activities such as yoga, tai chi, or water aerobics are offered in many towns. With the bonus of social connection, these sessions provide an organized method of being active.

8. **Seniors Should** be encouraged to create reasonable and attainable exercise objectives. Whether it's taking more steps each day, going to a certain amount of fitness classes each week, or taking up a new sport, achieving objectives gives you a feeling of direction and success.

Seniors may ensure that remaining active becomes a pleasurable and sustainable part of their lifestyle by implementing these measures into their routine, which will allow them to effortlessly combine physical exercise with social engagement. Social networks' support and friendship will serve as motivators for an active and healthy lifestyle.

Reduced Stress

Seniors who participate in social activities benefit greatly from it, as it provides them with a feeling of stability and emotional fortitude. Here's a detailed explanation of how making meaningful relationships may reduce stress:

1. **Prioritize Social Time:** To start, make social time a priority in your weekly or daily schedule. Set aside time regularly to catch up with friends—in person, on the

phone, or online. Stress resilience is built on a foundation of consistent social involvement.

2. **Create a Network of Supportive Friends:** Nurture a network of friends who have similar interests and beliefs. These relationships provide a safety net during trying times by providing a forum for sharing worries and getting support and understanding.

3. **Take Part in Group Activities:** Take part in clubs or group activities that relate to your interests. Participating in shared activities, such as reading clubs, gardening groups, or community organizations, may foster camaraderie and provide respite from daily tensions.

4. **Engage in Meaningful Discussions** while practicing active listening. A sense of connection and understanding is fostered when friends share their ideas and emotions. This conversation provides an emotional release, which lessens the tension.

5. **Seek Emotional Assistance:** Don't be afraid to ask dependable pals for emotional assistance while you're under stress. It is reassuring to know that there are people out there who genuinely care and are willing to lend an ear.

6. **Set Healthful Limits:** Acquire the skill of setting healthful limits in interpersonal interactions. Stress-inducing confrontations are less likely to occur when there is clear communication about expectations and personal boundaries. This keeps social interactions constructive and encouraging.

7. **Use Stress-reduction Strategies:** Include stress-reduction strategies in social gatherings. Exercises that promote social interaction and general stress reduction, such as yoga, meditation, and relaxation sessions, also improve the social experience.

8. **Promote Joy and Laughter:** Give priority to things that make you happy and laugh. Laughter is a recognized stress reliever and mood enhancer, whether it is experienced via lighthearted activities, amusing discussions, or shared interests.

Seniors may build a strong barrier against stress by deliberately incorporating social contact into their lives by following these steps. Seniors who have meaningful relationships and the support of friends are better able to manage pressures that may emerge in many areas of their lives and feel more secure and resilient emotionally.

Increase Happiness

Seniors who keep up an active social life report higher levels of happiness, which is indicative of the beneficial effects of social interactions on mental and emotional health. Here's a step-by-step tutorial on how to make meaningful relationships and increase happiness:

1. **Build Positive Connections:** To begin with, build positive connections with people who inspire and encourage you. The foundation for greater happiness is created by surrounding oneself with pleasant and helpful companions who have similar ideals.

2. **Encourage Meaningful Connections:** Make it a priority to connect with others who share your interests

by becoming involved in activities that suit your hobbies. This might include going to events, joining clubs, or becoming a member of organizations that share interests to provide a feeling of satisfaction and purpose.

3. **Celebrate Milestones and Shared Achievements:** With friends, commemorate shared accomplishments. Recognizing group achievements makes success even more joyful and fosters a feeling of contentment among those involved, which helps maintain a positive outlook.

4. **Take Part in Recreational Activities:** Get your buddies involved in some active leisure activities. Playing games, going on trips, or engaging in hobbies with others creates enduring memories and lifts the spirits of those around you.

5. **Express Gratitude:** Make it a practice to thank people in your social groups. Expressing gratitude and thanks to others improves relationships and creates a positive atmosphere that raises happiness levels.

6. **Make Social Time a Priority:** Schedule a regular time for socializing. Regular social interaction, whether it takes the form of a virtual meeting, coffee date, or weekly get-together, establishes a rhythm of connection that supports long-term enjoyment.

7. **Examine Mindfulness Techniques** with friends by engaging in joint mindfulness practice. Incorporating mindfulness into social activities, whether via group meditation, nature walks, or relaxation sessions,

improves self-awareness and promotes a calmer, more satisfied state of mind.

8. **Promote Playfulness and Laughter:** Give priority to activities that promote playfulness and laughter. Laughing together has a positive effect on happiness and mood, creating a setting where laughing becomes a normal component of social interactions.

Seniors may actively increase their happiness levels by implementing these techniques into their social life. Maintaining significant social relationships throughout one's elderly years may lead to a more enjoyable and rewarding existence, as seen by the laughter, adventures, and feeling of camaraderie shared by these individuals.

Better Cognitive Performance

Seniors who regularly engage in social interactions have improvements in their cognitive performance. The brain is stimulated by social interactions, intellectual debates, and conversations, which may lower the risk of cognitive decline and increase cognitive flexibility. Here's a detailed explanation of how making meaningful social ties might improve cognitive function:

1. **Take Part in Intellectual Conversations:** Actively participate in conversations about ideas with friends. Engaging in thought-provoking discussions improves cognitive performance, whether the topics are current affairs, personal experiences, or common interests.

2. **Join Study Groups or Book Clubs:** Participating in study groups or book clubs provides organized environments for intellectual discussion. In addition to

stimulating the intellect, reading books, evaluating literature, and taking part in educational debates also promote a feeling of camaraderie.

3. **Adopt a Lifelong Learning Attitude:** Foster an attitude of lifelong learning. Attend seminars, online courses, or workshops that fit your interests. Not only does ongoing education increase one's knowledge base, but it also keeps the mind sharp and interested.

4. **Engage in Brain Games:** Integrate mental exercises into conversational gatherings. Playing games like chess, crosswords, or other cognitive activities with others brings a pleasant element that enhances mental workouts and fosters cognitive agility.

5. **Attend Cultural Events:** Take part in cultural activities or take your friends to museums. Cognitive stimulation is achieved by exposure to novel concepts, artistic expressions, and cultural events, which broadens one's perspective and fosters creativity.

6. **Attend Church Events:** Your church community is an excellent source and place to meet old friends, make new connections, and participate in church events. Here you will at least meet people who have similar beliefs as yourself.

7. **Promote Debates and Conversations:** Promote debates and conversations among friends and family. Exploring diverse viewpoints and thought-provoking concepts enhances cognitive adaptation and resilience when confronted with cognitive difficulties.

8. **Make Connections with Diverse People:** Try to make connections with people who have different experiences and backgrounds. Engaging with others who possess diverse opinions expands one's cognitive frontiers and helps the brain adjust to new concepts and points of view.

9. **Engage in Mindfulness and Meditation:** Incorporate these practices into social interactions. By encouraging concentration, attention, and emotional management, mindful techniques improve cognitive performance and brain health in general.

Seniors may take advantage of the cognitive advantages of meaningful relationships by deliberately implementing these procedures into their social interactions. In addition to stimulating the brain, conversing, thinking, and participating in social activities also help maintain cognitive flexibility, which lowers the risk of cognitive decline and fosters long-term cognitive well-being.

Decreased Risk of Mental Decline

One important element linked to a lower risk of mental decline in seniors is the maintenance of strong social relationships. Long-term mental health is promoted by the mental stimulation that comes from social involvement, which plays a vital role in maintaining cognitive capacities. Here's how to use deep social ties to actively lower the danger of mental deterioration step-by-step:

1. **Put Frequent Social Interaction First:** Give frequent social interaction top attention in your day-to-day activities. Make time for social interactions with friends, family, and neighbors to establish a regular

social engagement rhythm that fosters cerebral stimulation.

2. **Join Social Clubs or Groups:** Participating in interest-based social clubs or groups offers supervised chances for consistent engagement. Through discussions and activities that are shared, these groups provide mental stimulation and help members feel like they belong.

3. **Attend Neighborhood Events:** Engage in conversation or gatherings in your neighborhood. These events provide seniors with a chance to socialize as well as expose them to a variety of activities that enhance their cognitive abilities.

4. **Take Part in Multigenerational Activities:** Look for opportunities to engage with people of varying ages in multigenerational settings. Seniors who engage with a diverse population can think more creatively and are exposed to a wider range of viewpoints.

5. **Promote Lifelong Learning:** Within social circles, foster an attitude that values lifelong learning. Take part in seminars, workshops, or group courses. Seeking information can lower the risk of mental decline by stimulating the brain.

6. **Use Technology for Social Connection:** If physical distance is an issue, use technology to maintain social connections with friends and family. Social media, internet platforms, and video conversations provide frequent channels of connection that fill in gaps and stimulate the mind.

7. **Take Part in Group Exercise Classes:** Attend group exercise sessions that encourage social connection in addition to physical exertion. Moving about and interacting with others improves mental health in general and lowers the chance of cognitive decline.

8. **Encourage Cognitive Difficulties:** In social contexts, promote cognitive difficulties. Take part in tasks that call for strategic planning, critical thinking, or problem-solving. These tasks lower the chance of cognitive decline and help to maintain cognitive skills.

Seniors may proactively lower their risk of mental deterioration by implementing these measures into their everyday routines. Maintaining cognitive function via regular social interaction does not only supports mental health but also enhances the golden years of life with a rich and satisfying quality of life.

Reduced Risk of Mental Health Problems

Seniors who place a high value on social contact have a markedly decreased risk of mental health problems. Positive mental health outlooks are fostered by social circles' emotional support, which serves as a preventive factor against mental health problems, including anxiety and depression. Here's how to use deep social relationships to actively reduce the risk of mental health problems, step-by-step:

1. **Create Regular Social Routines:** Creating regular social routines guarantees that you will see your friends and family regularly. Regular social interaction— whether it takes the form of a virtual meeting, a coffee

date, or a weekly get-together—becomes a stabilizing element in preserving mental health.

2. **Cultivate Strong Emotional Relationships:** Give special attention to fostering strong emotional relationships among friends and family. Developing open lines of communication and trust with friends creates a solid support network that lessens susceptibility to mental health issues.

3. **Encourage Members of Social** groups to share their personal experiences. Open communication about emotions and difficulties fosters empathy and understanding, which lessens the isolation that may exacerbate mental health problems.

4. **Seek Professional Assistance Jointly:** Seek professional assistance jointly if necessary. Encouraging friends to go to therapy or counseling together may reduce stigma, create a caring atmosphere, and proactively address mental health issues.

5. **Take Part in Group Therapy or Support Groups:** Joining groups designed to address certain mental health issues or group therapy offers a forum for sharing experiences. Group environments provide collective support and normalize personal problems.

6. **Take Part in Stress-reducing Activities:** Get friends involved in stress-relieving activities. Together, these methods—whether they be mindfulness exercises, relaxation methods, or well-being-promoting social activities—help people become less stressed and have improved mental health.

7. **Promote Healthy Lifestyle Choices:** Encourage others in your social groups to lead healthy lifestyles. Encourage one another to continue eating healthily, exercising often, and getting enough sleep—all of which are essential for maintaining mental well-being.

8. **Establish a Supportive Environment:** Establish an atmosphere where people are at ease sharing their feelings. Emotional well-being is improved, and the likelihood of mental health problems is decreased in social circles when judgment is removed and acceptance is encouraged.

Seniors may prevent mental health problems by actively implementing these procedures in their social lives. The emotional support that comes from having strong social ties may act as a formidable barrier against mental health issues like depression and anxiety, improving mental well-being and building resilience in the face of adversity.

The importance of social connection becomes evident as we traverse the latter stages of life, as expressed in The Legacy of Farmington (n.d.), and the perspectives of Forbes (n.d.), and the Berkeley Greater Good Science Center. Encouraging a feeling of belonging goes beyond the typical, weaving emotional support into a complex tapestry. The social fiber of interaction and the rhythm of leading an active lifestyle blend to create a dynamic story that resonates across the pathways of our health. There is a noticeable lack of tension during these peaceful times, in favor of the harmonizing buzz of happiness. Raising happiness to a crescendo harmonizes with the cerebral rhythm, promoting mental health. This complex relationship, steered by the ties that bind us together, is a sturdy defense against the turmoil of mental illness and a stronghold against the darkness of mental illness. As the story comes to an end, revelations from Forbes, the Greater Good Science Center, and The Legacy of Farmington emphasize the critical role that social ties play in older citizens' well-being.

Building and Maintaining Social Connections

Retirement is a momentous time in life, and in the middle of seeking leisure and pleasure, social relationships are crucial. As discussed in the Retire Guide's insights (n.d.), establishing and preserving these relationships turn into essential elements of a happy retirement. People's search for new social connections takes them along a variety of paths, each of which presents a different opportunity for making connections. At the same time, careful techniques are necessary for the delicate art of maintaining established partnerships. This thorough guide explores where new social ties might be formed and provides advice on how to foster and sustain these important relationships. It follows the principles described in the Retire Guide (n.d.). supplementary viewpoints from the United States and the Second Wind Movement (n.d.). News & World Report (2017) adds more knowledge, resulting in a comprehensive manual for retirees looking for a lively social life.

Creating and sustaining social ties is essential to a happy retirement. This is a thorough guide that draws on knowledge from the Retire Guide and other sources:

1. **Where can you meet people in the social media age?**

- **Community Centers and Groups:** Look into community centers in your area or sign up for groups that share your interests. These hubs often hold a variety of events and activities, offering chances to network with new individuals who have similar interests.

- **Volunteer Organizations:** Volunteer for issues that you are passionate about. In addition to helping the community, volunteering brings people together with peers who share their enthusiasm for changing the world.

- **Educational Courses:** Sign up for seminars or courses that are educational. Acquiring novel abilities or exploring captivating topics not only challenges the intellect but also provides an opportunity to establish relationships with other students.

- **Social Media and Online Groups:** Make use of social media sites and online communities to establish connections with others who have similar interests or life experiences. Expanding social circles and making new acquaintances is made simple by virtual communities.

- **Local events and gatherings:** Participate in regional fairs, events, or get-togethers. These events provide a laid-back environment for meeting new individuals in the neighborhood, and creating relationships that may develop into something more in the future.

2. **How do you keep up your present social networks?**

- ○ **Frequent Contact:** Give your current friends and acquaintances priority when it comes to frequent contact. Regular communication, whether via phone conversations, video chats, or in-person encounters, fosters deep bonds.

- ○ **Arrange Group Activities:** Arrange get-togethers or excursions with friends. Whether it's a hiking trip, reading club, or monthly lunch, shared experiences generate enduring memories and cement relationships.

- ○ **Celebrate Milestones:** Honor and commemorate significant anniversaries in friends' lives. Celebrating milestones like birthdays, anniversaries, and personal successes together promotes a feeling of community and support.

- ○ **Provide Support During Difficulties:** Be there for friends when they need you the most. Assisting, whether it is material or emotional, strengthens the bond between the two people and fosters a feeling of security in the social bond.

- ○ **Plan Reunions:** Plan get-togethers or reunions with former acquaintances. Making new connections with people you used to know not only brings back happy memories but also gives you a chance to catch up and deepen relationships.

- ○ **Partaking in Common Interests and Hobbies:** Take part in common interests and hobbies. Engaging in hobbies or pastimes together, such as crafts, athletics, or gardening, brings life to the partnership.

○ **Show Your Gratitude:** Show your appreciation for having pals in your life. Making the effort to express gratitude helps to sustain the connection by reaffirming its worth.

○ **Keep an Open Mind to New Connections:** While preserving current relationships, keep an open mind to new ones. Adopting a wide social network guarantees a steady stream of new ideas and enriches life. Also, remember that it is never too late to create new contacts.

Through the active implementation of these tactics, retirees may create new social networks and strengthen those they already have, resulting in a vibrant social life that improves their retirement years in general. Extra information from the United States and the Second Wind Movement. News & World Report offers insightful advice on how to maintain and strengthen social ties after retirement.

Social ties are the threads that weave a story of common experiences, friendship, and emotional support into the fabric of retirement. The information obtained from Retire Guide (n.d.) emphasizes how important it is to make deliberate attempts to build new relationships as well as value those that already exist. As the article points out, seniors might go out on a quest to meet new people in volunteer environments, community centers, educational settings, and even online. At the same time, social connection maintenance is an art that requires meaningful gestures, regular contact, and time-bound shared activities. The extra knowledge from the U.S. and the Second Wind Movement (n.d.) enhances this story. News & World Report (2017) offers insightful advice that adds subtle levels to the skill of creating and maintaining social relationships during retirement. The relationships retirees build offer not just a company but also a deep sense of purpose and well-being as they traverse this stage of life.

A Story: Harmony of New Beginnings

Mark missed the lively symphony of his coworkers amid the peaceful morning of retirement, the comforting rhythm of their shared laughter resonating in his mind. He felt alone, like a lonely note in a quiet chamber, as he made the shift from the regimented regularity of the workplace to the unknown realm of retirement.

One day, Mark was browsing Reddit's virtual retirement experience section when he came across a post that expressed exactly how he felt. The stories of others struck a chord, offering a solace-giving tune of common hardships and just-discovered melodies. Motivated by the collective knowledge, Mark chose to write his happy song.

Entering the neighborhood, he took on the task of creating a new social circle with courage. Serving others started to be seen as the first instrument that struck the chords of connection and purpose. He met a harmony of like-minded people via neighborhood gatherings and charitable causes; each note added richness to his newfound symphony.

Unfazed, Mark pursued a variety of paths and joined groups that shared his interests. Each association, whether it was a reading club or a gardening club, contributed notes to the composition of his retirement life. In little time at all, the lonely note became a lively chorus of friendship and common interests.

As the days went by, Mark discovered that he was in charge of this cohesive group, setting the pace for his brand-new neighborhood. The warmth of companionship replaced the sense of solitude like mist in the morning. He became the composer of his fate, layering notes of camaraderie and intention into a lovely arrangement of retirement.

The melody of new beginnings had become his retirement anthem, a testament to the transformative power of embracing change and conducting one's life into a beautiful symphony of possibilities. In the last act of his story, Mark found comfort in the words of Germany Kent, *"Never underestimate the power you have to take your life in a new direction."*

Transition: As we reach the end of this incredible journey, we want to take a moment to remind you of all the valuable insights and knowledge you have gained. Our conclusion page will summarize all the information you have learned, making it easy for you to create a happy and successful retirement.

We wish you an enjoyable reading and look forward to seeing you on the next page.

Conclusion

It gives me great pleasure to see you get here after reading the Retirement Planning: One Size Does Not Fit All: A Holistic Essential Guide for Every Lifestyle! This is a remarkable accomplishment since many people are still unaware that retirement planning starts today and not tomorrow. Let's take time to review and honor the abundance of information that you have gained over this incredible journey:

- **The 3 Big Retirement Questions:** Individuals went into the three crucial questions that define the threshold of retirement in the chapter that came before this one. They conducted a retrospective analysis of the challenges that are associated with the appropriate retirement age, the financial foundation that is required for a pleasant retirement, and the methods that are essential to providing continuous financial security after retirement. It was determined that careful contemplation and preparation were necessary and that they formed the foundation for a successful retirement.

- **Financial Foundation—Budgeting:** The Financial Foundation After completing the preliminary considerations, attention switched to the most important aspect of retirement planning, which is the creation of a budget. At this point, people took the initiative to participate in the laborious process of developing budgets that were grounded in reality. These financial plans considered both existing and potential expenditures, and they advised on how to effectively manage expenditures, prudently save money, and build a solid financial foundation. A strong emphasis was placed on the critical role that budgeting plays in maintaining financial discipline and avoiding frequent errors that might put retirement security at risk.

- **Turning Spare Time into Cash:** The process of turning spare time into cash began when the prospect of retirement drew near. This led to the investigation of innovative ways to generate revenue. The purpose of this chapter was to explore the concepts of using one's abilities and free time to produce more revenue. Among the things that were considered were chances for part-time jobs, freelance work, and the turning of hobbies into earnings streams. The story stressed how important it is to maintain an active lifestyle and participate in activities that are significant to oneself while simultaneously increasing one's income during retirement.

- **Retirement Investment Strategies:** Retirees, in the course of an exhaustive investigation, examined a variety of investment strategies that were specifically adapted to their upcoming retirement. There was a shift in the focus of research to include stocks, bonds, and real estate, along with insights into the risk and return characteristics of each of these asset classes. The purpose of this chapter was to shed light on the fundamental principles of diversification, risk tolerance, and the need for recalibration of investment strategies as retirement approaches. The ultimate goal was to achieve a harmonic balance between growth and security during retirement.

- **One More Simple Investment Strategy—Index Funds:** Following a more in-depth exploration of the complexities of investing, attention was directed to a particular method known as index funds. The complexities of the idea were explored, and you gained an appreciation for the benefits that are inherent in these funds. Index funds have developed as pillars that help retirees search for a clear but powerful investing plan. These pillars included the simplicity of index funds, their wide market exposure, and their cost-effectiveness.

- **Health is Wealth:** The symbiotic link between health and financial well-being in retirement was the primary focus of this chapter. The phrase "health is wealth" was used to describe this relationship. Examining the influence that one's health has on the costs associated with retirement brought to light the need to make complete plans for one's healthcare. The deep relationship that exists between health and wealth was brought to light by the dissemination of information on the maintenance of a healthy lifestyle, the consideration of possibilities for long-term care, and the preparedness to deal with future healthcare bills after retirement.

- **The 5 Stages of Retirement—Stage 1:** Throughout many phases, starting with Stage 1, the transition from working to retiring was carried out. The participants shared their thoughts on the necessary changes, both emotionally and financially, that were necessary during this early period. To successfully traverse this fundamental stage, it was necessary to consider adaptation techniques since the psychological transition from a regimented professional life to a leisure-oriented life presented several problems.

- **The 5 Stages of Retirement—Stages 2–5:** We resumed our investigation of the phases of retirement, digging further into the ever-changing requirements and difficulties that come with each step. Several topics were brought up throughout the conversation, including altering priorities, anticipated changes in health, and alterations to living arrangements. The provision of actionable guidance on the management of the myriad facets that comprise retirement life contributed to the development of a comprehensive grasp of the dynamic path that retirees began.

- **Technical Navigation in Retirement:** The junction of technology and retirement was revealed when people investigated the function of technology in their post-working years. This was referred to as "Technical Navigation in Retirement." There was an investigation into the potential advantages, which included everything from social ties to healthcare and financial management. Concerns that are often associated with technology were addressed, and advice was given on how to embrace and navigate the constantly changing technological scene when one is retired. Safety practices and how to deal with scammers were also discussed.

- **Building and Nurturing Social Networks in Retirement:** In the last chapter, the focus shifted to the utmost importance of maintaining social relationships throughout retirement. At the same time, as the influence of social contacts on mental and emotional well-being was taken into consideration, several strategies for developing and maintaining a healthy social network were investigated. The final note of this in-depth investigation was the need to make conscious efforts to cultivate meaningful connections and to participate in community activities after retirement.

A Wealth of Retirement Strategies for Your Lifestyle

Because we are about to begin to practicalize this informative trip of Retirement Planning, it is time to use your substantial expertise. When it comes to retirement planning, the terrain is enormous, which includes a multitude of possibilities and infinite potential. You will be able to stimulate growth, inspire innovation, and position yourself as a visionary leader in the finance-driven retirement environment if you integrate this financial intelligence into your retirement plan in a seamless manner.

From Me to You

As you are about to close this exhilarating journey of individualized retirement planning, I strongly urge you to make use of the newly acquired information that you have obtained from our comprehensive Guide. Your capacity to manage the complexities of retirement planning may not only transform your own life, but it will also have a dramatic effect on the lives of people who fall within your sphere of influence for the better. Through the dissemination of information on this priceless resource, you can ensure that the knowledge gained will serve as a guiding light for others in their pursuit of a retirement that is driven by their specific financial situation.

You may want to think about being a catalyst for change in the landscape of retirement planning by sharing your valuable thoughts with the world. Your review on websites such as Amazon or at your preferred bookstore might act as a beacon, pointing folks in the direction of their journey to retirement enlightenment. We would like to extend our congratulations on accomplishing this remarkable objective. With this Guide by your side, the options for developing a retirement plan that is suited to your interests are almost limitless.

In the world of retirement planning, which is driven by finances, I would like to toast your achievements, your endless potential, and the boundless opportunities waiting for you.

With best wishes,
Skylar Waves

Pay It Forward By Passing On The Baton

Title: **Keeping the Game of Retirement Alive**

Now that you have everything you need to successfully plan your golden retirement, it's time to pass on your newfound knowledge and show other readers where they can find the same help.

Simply by leaving your honest opinion of this book on Amazon, you'll show other retirees where they can find the information they're looking for and pass your passion for retirement forward.

Thank you for your help. The "Retirement Planning: One Size Does Not Fit All" is kept alive when we pass on our knowledge—and you're helping us to do just that.

Please *click here* or scan the QR Code below to leave your review.

Best regards,
Skylar Waves

Glossary

With the help of these enlightening glossaries, take a voyage through the dynamic world of financial markets and investing knowledge. Discovering the S&P 500's resiliency or comprehending the subtle differences between index funds, ETFs, and mutual funds—each glossary serves as a doorway to financial wisdom. Discover the ideas that the renowned Warren Buffett supports, as well as the calculated measures to take to register an online brokerage account or take advantage of Robo-advisors' efficiency.

These glossaries provide the essential knowledge needed to successfully navigate the complex stock market and make wise choices that will lead to a healthy financial future, regardless of experience level:

Adjunct Professor: An adjunct professor is a part-time instructor at a university who is not on a tenure track. They often bring real-world expertise to the classroom.

Affiliate Marketing: A performance-based marketing strategy where individuals earn a commission for promoting other companies' products or services.

Asset Adjustment Strategy: A financial approach that involves aligning retirement savings with current income, considering potential lifestyle changes and fluctuations in income over the retirement years.

Automatic Payroll Deductions: Automatic payroll deductions are contributions to retirement accounts that are deducted directly from an individual's paycheck, ensuring consistency in savings habits.

Beyond Impulse Story: Lily's journey from impulsive shopping to financial serenity, highlighting the transformative power of self-awareness, the 24-hour rule, and support from online communities.

Buffett's Endorsement of Index Funds: Warren Buffett supports index funds based on principles such as the lack of need for special skills, preference for passive investing, emphasis on low fees, and consistent long-term investing. His endorsement highlights the value of disciplined, patient investing over attempting to beat the market.

Content Monetization: Earning money by creating and sharing valuable content through channels like blogs, YouTube, or social media.

Compound Growth: Compound growth is the process where investments generate earnings, and those earnings generate more earnings in subsequent periods.

Contribution Limits: Contribution limits refer to the maximum amount individuals can contribute to their retirement accounts in a given year. Please visit irs.gov for current contribution limits if you reside in the USA or your local tax agency if you are outside of the USA.

Debt to Freedom Story: The tale of Emma, Jack, and Maya overcoming financial challenges by prioritizing debt repayment and building emergency funds, demonstrating the power of commitment to financial wellness.

Diversification: Spreading investments across different assets to reduce risk and optimize returns.

Dow Jones Industrial Average (DJIA): The oldest and most well-known stock market indexes.

Dropshipping: An e-commerce model where the seller does not hold inventory, and products are shipped directly from the supplier to the customer.

Exchange Traded Funds (ETFs): A security which can be bought on an exchange.

Employer Matching Contributions: Employer matching contributions are contributions made by employers to a retirement account, often matching a portion of the employee's contributions.

Entrepreneurial Spirit: The mindset and qualities characterized by innovation, risk-taking, and a proactive approach to business endeavors.

Financial Independence: Financial independence is the state where an individual has enough wealth to sustain their desired lifestyle without relying on traditional employment.

Financial Acumen: Financial acumen refers to the ability to understand and make informed decisions about financial matters.

Financial Preparedness: The state of having sufficient savings, investments, and income to support a comfortable lifestyle during retirement, often assessed by evaluating one's monthly and annual income needs.

Flexible Retirement Planning: An approach that emphasizes adaptability in retirement plans, acknowledging that goals, interests, and financial needs may evolve over time, requiring adjustments for a fulfilling retirement.

Freelance Consulting: Providing expert advice or services to clients on a temporary or project basis.

Financial Independence: Achieving a state where an individual has enough wealth and resources to sustain their desired lifestyle without relying on traditional employment.

401(k): A 401(k) is a popular employer-sponsored retirement plan known for its employer contributions, tax deferral, and higher contribution limits.

Solo 401(k) (Individual 401(k)): This is for self-employed business owners who have no employees but it can be used to cover their spouses.

Gig Economy: The gig economy refers to a job market characterized by short-term, flexible, and freelance work arrangements.

Good Versus Bad Debt: Distinguishing between debts that contribute to wealth-building (good debt) and those with negative impacts on financial health (bad debt), emphasizing the importance of minimizing bad debt.

Index Fund: An index fund is a passive investment vehicle designed to replicate the performance of a specific market index, providing diversified exposure to a basket of securities that mirror the index. Investors often choose index funds for their low-cost advantage, broad diversification, and suitability for long-term investment.

Individual Retirement Account (IRA): A tax-advantaged investment account allowing individuals to save for retirement, with variations like Traditional and Roth IRAs.

Impulse Spending: Exploring the impact of uncontrolled impulsive buying on long-term financial stability and retirement plans, with strategies such as the 24-hour rule and non-materialistic alternatives.

Importance of an Emergency Fund: The significance of maintaining an emergency fund to avoid high-interest debt, reduce financial stress, and recommend fund sizes ranging from three to six months of living expenses.

Importance of an Emergency Fund: Reinforcing the crucial role of an emergency fund in preventing high-interest debt, reducing financial stress, and providing a financial cushion for unexpected events.

Keep It Simple, Stupid (KISS): Indicates that although there are several types of retirement investment, this Guide will only use a streamlined approach.

Market Research: The process of gathering, analyzing, and interpreting information about a market, including potential customers and competitors.

Market Viability: Market viability refers to the potential of a product or service to meet the demands and expectations of the market.

Matching 401(k) Contributions: Matching 401(k) contributions refers to the practice where employers match a percentage of an employee's contributions to their 401(k) plan.

Monthly Income Benchmark: The recommended target, often set at around 80 percent of pre-retirement monthly income, is used to estimate the required income for a comfortable retirement.

Minimum Required Distributions (MRDs): Minimum required distributions are the minimum amount individuals must withdraw from their retirement accounts starting at age 72.

Necessity of Tracking Expenses: Stressing the importance of meticulous expense tracking for informed decision-making, using budgeting apps, and identifying areas for optimization to improve financial well-being.

Negative Effects of Too Much Bad Debt: Exploring the adverse consequences of excessive bad debt, including reduced savings, impaired credit scores, and limitations on financial flexibility.

Necessity of Tracking Expenses: Emphasizing the proactive role of expense tracking in achieving financial goals, using technology like budgeting apps, and forming a consistent tracking habit.

Negative Effects of Too Much Bad Debt: Delving into the detrimental impacts of excessive bad debt on savings, credit scores, and overall financial flexibility.

Needs and Wants: The fundamental distinction between necessities for survival (needs) and desires for pleasure and leisure (wants) in personal finance, emphasizing the importance of mindful spending and the 50/30/20 rule.

Niche Market: A specialized segment of the market for a particular kind of product or service.

Online Brokerage Account: An online brokerage account allows individuals to invest in various financial instruments, including index funds, through digital platforms provided by companies like Fidelity or Vanguard. Opening an online brokerage account is a strategic step for those entering the world of index fund investing.

Part-Time Engagement: In retirement, the practice of working part-time to supplement income, stay connected, and explore new interests or career paths.

Part-Time Employment for Retirees: Job opportunities suitable for individuals who have retired but seek part-time work.

Passion-Based Entrepreneurship: Building a business around one's passions and interests, aligning personal fulfillment with financial growth.

Passive Income: Earnings that require minimal effort or time from the earner, often generated from investments or rental properties.

Rental Property Income: Earning money by leasing out real estate properties to tenants, generating passive income.

Retirement Planning: The process of strategically preparing for one's post-career life, involving considerations such as financial security, housing choices, and lifestyle preferences.

Retirement Destination Factors: Critical considerations, including moving costs, cost of living, proximity to family and friends, climate, social life, and healthcare facilities, should be considered when choosing a location for retirement.

Risk Tolerance: Risk tolerance is the degree to which an individual is willing to accept variability in investment returns without becoming nervous or making impulsive decisions.

Riches Reimagined Story: A narrative comparing the extravagant spending of Johnny Depp with the philanthropic choices of Bill Gates, prompting reflections on the true essence of wealth and the impact of stewardship on the world.

Retirement Savings—10 to 15 percent Rule of Thumb: A rule of thumb suggests allocating 10 to 15 percent of income for retirement savings, acknowledging the need for customization based on individual circumstances.

Retirement Planning: The process of setting financial goals and creating strategies to ensure a comfortable retirement.

Resilience in Market Volatility: Resilience in market volatility refers to the ability of an investment, like the S&P 500, to withstand and recover from downturns or adverse economic events. The S&P 500 has demonstrated resilience, bouncing back from significant market downturns.

Robo-Advisors: Robo-advisors are digital platforms that use algorithms to automate investment management. They offer low-cost, accessible, and personalized investment strategies. Examples include Betterment and Schwab Intelligent Portfolios.

Rollovers: Rollovers are the transfer of funds from one retirement account to another without triggering taxes or penalties.

SEP IRA (Simplified Employee Pension IRA): A SEP IRA is a retirement plan for self-employed individuals and small businesses. It offers ease of administration, employer contributions, and flexible contribution limits.

Similarities Among Index Funds, ETFs, and Mutual Funds: Index funds, ETFs, and mutual funds share commonalities in terms of objectives, structure, costs, and diversification benefits. Understanding these similarities helps investors make informed choices based on their preferences and strategies.

Selecting an Index Fund: Selecting an index fund involves evaluating factors such as expense ratios, management fees, tracking accuracy, fund size, and historical performance. Choosing an index fund tailored to one's goals and risk tolerance is crucial for successful long-term investing.

S&P 500 Index Funds Comparison: Comparing different S&P 500 index funds based on criteria like expense ratios, management fees, historical performance, and tracking accuracy. Investors explore and compare S&P 500 index funds to make informed decisions aligned with their financial objectives.

S&P 500: The S&P 500 is a market-capitalization-weighted index that comprises 500 of the largest publicly traded companies in the United States. It serves as a benchmark for assessing the overall performance of the U.S. stock market.

SMART Goals: SMART goals are specific, measurable, attainable, relevant, and time-bound goals that help individuals set and achieve meaningful objectives.

Smart Goal Setting for Retirement: Smart goal setting for retirement is the process of setting specific, measurable, attainable, relevant, and time-bound goals to enhance retirement savings strategies.

Social Security: A government program that provides financial assistance to retirees and certain disabled individuals, contributing to their overall retirement income.

Solo 401(k) (Individual 401(k)): A solo 401(k), also known as an individual 401(k), is designed for self-employed individual business owners. It allows for higher contribution limits, both employer and employee contributions, and flexible investment options.

Simplicity of the 50/30/20 Rule: An easy-to-follow budgeting rule dividing income into needs, wants, and savings, providing a straightforward approach to financial planning for both short-term and long-term goals.

Strategies to Reduce Debt: Practical approaches to reduce debt, including creating a budget, prioritizing repayments using methods like snowball or avalanche, debt consolidation, and increasing income while cutting expenses.

Strategies to Reduce Debt: Providing actionable strategies to reduce debt, including budget creation, repayment methods, debt consolidation, and a focus on increasing income while cutting expenses.

Stock Market Investments: The act of buying and holding financial instruments like stocks, bonds, or mutual funds to generate returns.

Tax Deferral: Tax deferral is the practice of delaying the payment of taxes on contributions and investment gains until withdrawal during retirement.

Tax Deductible Contributions: Tax-deductible contributions are contributions to retirement accounts that are deductible from the individual's taxable income, providing an immediate tax benefit.

Tax Efficiency: Tax efficiency refers to maximizing tax benefits and minimizing tax liability in financial planning, including retirement savings.

The 50/30/20 Rule: A budgeting guideline that suggests allocating 50 percent of income to needs, 30 percent to wants, and 20 percent to savings and debt repayment, promoting a balanced financial approach for stability and enjoyment.

Traditional IRA: A traditional IRA is a personal retirement account that offers tax-deductible contributions, tax-deferred growth, and a wide range of investment choices.

Volunteerism in Retirement: The act of contributing time and skills to meaningful causes during retirement, providing personal fulfillment, and making a positive impact on society.

Warren Buffett: Warren Buffett, also known as the Oracle of Omaha, is a highly successful investor and Chairman/CEO of Berkshire Hathaway. He is known for his value investing approach, which emphasizes simplicity, long-term strategies, and the importance of low fees.

Wide Investment Choices: Wide investment choices refer to retirement accounts that offer a diverse range of investment options, providing individuals with control over their portfolios.

As we come to the end of our financial education journey, keep in mind that investing is both an art and a science. The glossaries have shown the S&P 500's tenacity, the ideas of Warren Buffett, and the variety of index funds and investing platforms available. Making well-informed decisions is crucial, whether you're attracted to the automation of Robo-advisors or the steadiness of index funds. May you approach investing with perseverance, self-control, and the steadfast conviction that, similar to the S&P 500's long-term prosperity, your financial objectives will eventually prosper. To a prosperous future filled with wealth!

References

Affiliate Marketing. (2023, March 21). *12 Proven Ways To Generate Multiple Streams Of Income*. LinkedIn. https://www.linkedin.com/pulse/12-proven-ways-generate-multiple-streams-income-affiliate-marketing

Any long term S&p 500 success stories? (2012). Reddit. https://www.reddit.com/r/stocks/comments/107gzqn/any_long_term_sp500_success_stories/

Benefits of sleep. (n.d.). health.gov. https://health.gov/myhealthfinder/healthy-living/mental-health-and-relationships/get-enough-sleep

Budgeting Quotes (29 quotes). (2015). Goodreads.com. https://www.goodreads.com/quotes/tag/budgeting

Budgeting tips to stop impulse spending. (n.d.). No More Debts. https://nomoredebts.org/budgeting/budgeting-tips-stop-impulse-spending

Building and maintaining social connections. (2022, Jun. 16). RetireGuide. https://www.retireguide.com/retirement-life-leisure/healthy-aging/social-connections/

Burnette, M. (2024, February 8). *Emergency Fund: What it Is and Why it Matters*. NerdWallet. https://www.nerdwallet.com/article/banking/emergency-fund-why-it-matters#:~:text

Burunov, P. (2019, January 31). *Don't Get Stuck in the Honeymoon Phase of Retirement.* AWM. https://ambassador.partners/resources/retirement-planning/the-honeymoon-phase-of-retirement/

Caring for your Mental Health. (2022, December). National Institute of Mental Health. https://www.nimh.nih.gov/health/topics/caring-for-your-mental-healthhttps://www.nimh.nih.gov/health/topics/caring-for-your-mental-health

CFI Team. (n.d.). *Robo-Advisors.* Corporate Finance Institute. https://corporatefinanceinstitute.com/resources/wealth-management/robo-advisors/

Curtis, G. (2024, February 15). *Approaching Retirement? Can You Answer These 6 Questions?* Investopedia. https://www.investopedia.com/articles/retirement/07/retirement-questions.asp

Dahl, D. (2022, September 8). *50 Health is Wealth Quotes To Help Prioritize Being Well.* Everyday Power. https://everydaypower.com/health-is-wealth-quotes/

Debt is often just a click away. (2023, November 30). Mayaonmoney.co.za. https://mayaonmoney.co.za/2023/11/how-social-media-can-encourage-overspending/

Dekker T. (n.d.). *Thomas dekker quotes.* BrainyQuote. https://www.brainyquote.com/quotes/thomas_dekker_204715

Di Mento, M. (2022, December 30). *Bill Gates made 2022's biggest charitable donation: $5 billion.* Los Angeles Times. https://www.latimes.com/business/story/2022-12-30/bill-gates-made-2022s-biggest-charitable-donation-5-billion

Dickinson, R. (n.d.). *6 critical questions to answer before planning your retirement.* Altus Financial. https://www.altusfinancial.com.au/blog/6-critical-questions-to-answer-before-planning-your-retirement

DiNuzzo, E. (2018, April 7). *The workouts 15 of your favorite celebrities do to stay in shape.* Business Insider. https://www.businessinsider.com/how-celebrities-work-out-2018-4?r=US&IR=T

Disney, W. (n.d.). *A quote by Walt Disney Company.* Goodreads. https://www.goodreads.com/quotes/31131-the-way-to-get-started-is-to-quit-talking-and

Dodds, C. (2024). *Britannica Money.* Britannica. https://www.britannica.com/money/what-is-the-50-30-20-rule

Downsizing or relocating as part of strategy. (2013). Reddit. https://www.reddit.com/r/retirement/comments/16of8jj/downsizing_or_relocating_as_part_of_st rategy/

Eating a balanced diet. (2013, April). NHS. https://www.nhs.uk/live-well/eat-well/how-to-eat-a-balanced-diet/eating-a-balanced-diet/

ESI. (2019, March 16). *What to Do with Your Time in Early Retirement.* ESI Money. https://esimoney.com/what-to-do-with-your-time-in-early-retirement/

Exercise and Physical Activity Ideas. (n.d.). Myhealth.alberta.ca. Retrieved February 22, 2024, from https://myhealth.alberta.ca/Health/Pages/conditions.aspx?hwid=aa165656&lang=en-ca

Exercise Quotes (425 quotes). (n.d.). Goodreads. https://www.goodreads.com/quotes/tag/exercise

Fay, B. (2012). *Good Debt vs. Bad Debt - Types of Good and Bad Debts.* Debt.org. https://www.debt.org/advice/good-vs-bad/

Fernando, J. (2021, December 11). *What is a 401(k) Plan?* Investopedia. https://www.investopedia.com/terms/1/401kplan.asp

Fernando, J. (2023, March 24). *What Are Index Funds, and How Do They Work?* Investopedia. https://www.investopedia.com/terms/i/indexfund.asp

Fifteen tips to become computer savvy at an older age. (January 2023). Aging.com. https://aging.com/15-tips-to-become-computer-savvy-at-an-older-age/

Fifty 30 20 rule: The realistic budget that actually works. (2022, August 12). N26.com. https://n26.com/en-eu/blog/50-30-20-rule

Four 01(k): should i only contribute what the company matches? (2021). Reddit. https://www.reddit.com/r/personalfinance/comments/ny55s3/401k_should_i_only_contribute_what_the_company/

Fowler, J. (2021b, September 30). *Why an emergency fund is important.* Investopedia. https://www.investopedia.com/financial-edge/0812/why-an-emergency-fund-is-important.aspx

Frankenfield, J. (2023, October 12). *Robo-Advisor (Robo-Adviser).* Investopedia. https://www.investopedia.com/terms/r/roboadvisor-roboadviser.asp

Good debt vs. Bad debt. (n.d.). Britannica. https://www.britannica.com/money/good-debt-vs-bad

Grant, K. (2017, June 9). *Ouch! 3 ways poor health hurts in retirement.* CNBC. https://www.cnbc.com/2017/06/09/3-ways-poor-health-hurts-in-retirement.html

Groth, L. (2023, November 29). *Tech Tips for Seniors: Master Your Devices and Make Tech Work for You.* Best Life. https://bestlifeonline.com/tech-tips-for-seniors-master-your-devices/

Has anyone else just accepted that retirement is not an option? (2013). Reddit. https://www.reddit.com/r/NoStupidQuestions/co mments/16kau03/has_anyone_else_just_accepte d_that_retirement_is/

Hays, A. (2015, August 20). *How to Plan for Multiple Financial Goals (without going crazy)*. Calculate My Wealth. https://calculatemywealth.com/how-to-plan-for-multiple-financial-goals/

Health is wealth quotes. (2022, March 04). Vantage Fit. https://www.vantagefit.io/blog/health-is-wealth-quotes/

Health is wealth quotes. (n.d.). AZ Quotes. https://www.azquotes.com/quotes/topics/health-is-wealth.html

Healthy diet. (2020, April 29). World Health Organization. https://www.who.int/news-room/fact-sheets/detail/healthy-diet

Healthy eating for a healthy weight. (n.d.). CDC. https://www.cdc.gov/healthyweight/healthy_eati ng/index.html

Healthy Eating. Simplified. (2019). Lifesum. https://lifesum.com/

Heiser, C. (2017, June 26). *16 ways to sleep better tonight*. NBC News. https://www.nbcnews.com/better/health/16-ways-get-better-night-s-sleep-without-popping-pill-ncna756311

Here's what happens when you retire with no savings. (2023, August 15). The Motley Fool. https://www.fool.com/the-ascent/buying-stocks/articles/heres-what-happens-when-you-retire-with-no-savings/

How can i stop impulse buying? (2013). Reddit. https://www.reddit.com/r/Anticonsumption/comments/u9k6wn/how_can_i_stop_impulse_buying/

How does a 401(k) plan work? (n.d.). Ameriprise. https://www.ameriprise.com/financial-goals-priorities/retirement/what-is-a-401k

How I found my passion and purpose in retirement. (2023, February 11). Sassy Sister Stuff. https://www.sassysisterstuff.com/how-i-found-my-passion-and-purpose-in-retirement/

How is your social friends circle now that you are retired? (n.d.). Reddit. https://www.reddit.com/r/retirement/comments/1298qkb/how_is_your_social_friends_circle_now_that_you/

How Johnny Depp spends $2 million a month. (2017, August 31). CNBC. https://www.cnbc.com/2017/08/31/how-johnny-depp-blows-2-million-a-month.html

How much of my income should I save every month? (n.d.). TIAA. https://www.tiaa.org/public/learn/personal-finance-101/how-much-of-my-income-should-i-save-every-month

How much should I save now to have enough when I retire? Understanding retirement. (n.d.). Discovery. https://www.discovery.co.za/corporate/how-much-should-i-save-for-when-i-retire

How much to save for retirement. (2023, June 27). NerdWallet. https://www.nerdwallet.com/article/investing/how-much-to-save-for-retirement

How to *budget: a step-by-step guide.* (2024, February 16). NerdWallet. https://www.nerdwallet.com/article/finance/how-to-budget

How to find your passion in retirement. (2024, Jan. 07). Retirement Tips and Tricks. https://retirementtipsandtricks.com/how-to-find-your-passion-in-retirement/

How to invest in index funds. (2024, February 01). The Motley Fool. https://www.fool.com/investing/how-to-invest/index-funds/

How to invest in index funds. (2024, January 31). NerdWallet. https://www.nerdwallet.com/article/investing/how-to-invest-in-index-funds

How to invest in index funds. (n.d.). Business Insider. https://www.businessinsider.com/personal-finance/how-to-invest-in-index-funds

How to separate wants and needs. (2022, June 20). The Balance. https://www.thebalancemoney.com/how-to-separate-wants-and-needs-453592

How to set retirement goals. (n.d.). Western & Southern Financial Group. https://www.westernsouthern.com/retirement/how-to-set-retirement-goals

How to stop impulse buys. (2023, Oct. 13). Ramsey solutions. https://www.ramseysolutions.com/budgeting/stop-impulse-buys

How to Tell the Difference Between Your Wants and Needs. (n.d.). Fairwinds Credit Union. https://www.fairwinds.org/articles/how-to-tell-the-difference-between-your-wants-and-needs

How to track monthly expenses. (2024, January 30). NerdWallet. https://www.nerdwallet.com/article/finance/tracking-monthly-expenses

I want to learn how to save money and stop impulse buying. (2013). Reddit. https://www.reddit.com/r/IWantToLearn/comments/uechpd/iwtl_how_to_save_money_and_stop_impulse_buying/

Important stages to consider when planning your retirement. (2023, May 29). Fanews. https://www.fanews.co.za/article/retirement/1357 /general/1358/important-stages-to-consider-when-planning-your-retirement/37114

Impulse buying. (n.d.). *What is it and how to avoid it.* Capital One. https://www.capitalone.com/learn-grow/money-management/impulse-buying/

Indeed Editorial Team. (2023, January 19). *11 part-time jobs for retired people to enhance your pension: 9 options to consider.* Indeed. https://uk.indeed.com/career-advice/finding-a-job/part-time-jobs-for-retired-people

Indeed Editorial Team. (2023, June 29). *12 Great Part-Time Jobs for After Retirement.* Indeed Career Guide. https://www.indeed.com/career-advice/finding-a-job/best-jobs-after-retirement

Index funds - I've only lost money. (2013). Reddit. https://www.reddit.com/r/Bogleheads/comments /17bnl28/index_funds_ive_only_lost_money/

Index funds. (2024, February, 01). The Motley Fool. https://www.fool.com/investing/how-to-invest/index-funds/

Is it normal if life gets boring when you're retired? (2013). Reddit. https://www.reddit.com/r/retirement/comments/ 149urrk/is_it_normal_if_life_gets_boring_when _youre/

Joad, U. (2022, November 22). *Wants vs. Needs: Understanding the Difference.* Fi.Money. https://fi.money/blog/posts/wants-vs-needs-understanding-the-difference

Joyce, L. (2023, April 28). *Top tips for creating a Retirement Vision Board.* LinkedIn. https://www.linkedin.com/pulse/top-tips-creating-retirement-vision-board-laura-joyce/

Kagan, J. (2021, February 18). *Phases of Retirement.* Investopedia. https://www.investopedia.com/terms/p/phases-retirement.asp

Kagan, J. (2021b, February 21). *Where Should I Retire?* Investopedia. https://www.investopedia.com/where-should-i-retire-7967363

Kent, G. (2023, January 12). *Never underestimate the power you have to take your life in a new direction.* Country Living. https://www.countryliving.com/life/g30337217/new-beginnings-quotes/

Knowledge at Wharton Staff. (2014, January 14). *The Retirement Problem: What to Do With All That Time?* Knowledge@Wharton. https://knowledge.wharton.upenn.edu/article/the-retirement-problem-what-will-you-do-with-all-that-time/

Krier, J. (2022b, December 13). *Here Are the 6 Biggest Side Hustle Mistakes to Avoid as a Newbie.*

Medium. https://jackkrier.medium.com/here-are-the-6-biggest-side-hustle-mistakes-to-avoid-as-a-newbie-70d655acb9fa

Leech, J. (2022, January 6). *10 reasons why good sleep is important.* Healthline. https://www.healthline.com/nutrition/10-reasons-why-good-sleep-is-important

Life after retirement. (n.d.). Nolo. https://www.nolo.com/legal-encyclopedia/life-after-retirement-30229.html

Living50. (2024, January 2). *Retirement vision board: Create.* Living50. https://www.living50.com/blog/retirement-vision-board-create

Mack, B. (2022, March 18). *How to Get Through the "Disenchantment" Phase of Retirement.* Cornerstone Wealth Management. https://www.cornerstonevegas.com/how-to-get-through-the-disenchantment-phase-of-retirement/

Marquit, M. (2020, June 15). *Retirement Basics: What Is A 401(k) Plan?* Forbes Advisor. https://www.forbes.com/advisor/retirement/what-is-401k/

Maverick, J.B. (2024, January 3). *What is the average annual return of the s&p 500?* Investopedia. https://www.investopedia.com/ask/answers/042415/what-average-annual-return-sp-500.asp

Meehan, H. G. (2021a, October 28). *41 Budget Quotes To Improve Your Budget!* Clever Girl Finance. https://www.clevergirlfinance.com/budget-quotes-to-budget-better/

Mraovic, J. (2021). *How to keep track of expenses.* Clockify Blog. https://clockify.me/blog/managing-tasks/expense-tracking/

MyFitnessPal. (2022). Myfitnesspal.com. https://www.myfitnesspal.com/

Navigating technology safely: tips for seniors. (2023, September 26). Senior Resource Connectors. https://seniorresourceconnectors.com/general/navigating-technology-safely-tips-for-seniors

NIH News in Health. (2013, April). *The benefits of slumber.* NIH. https://newsinhealth.nih.gov/2013/04/benefits-slumber

Nine inspiring budgeting quotes and how you can use them to take action now. (n.d.). Atypical Finance. https://www.atypicalfinance.com/9-inspiring-budgeting-quotes-and-how-you-can-use-them-to-take-action-now/

Nine mistakes to avoid when starting a side hustle. (2021, July 19). The Motley Fool. https://www.fool.com/the-ascent/personal-finance/articles/9-mistakes-to-avoid-when-starting-a-side-hustle/

Online Trading - Fidelity. (n.d.). Fidelity.com. Retrieved February 21, 2024, from https://www.fidelity.com/trading/online-trading

Online trading. (n.d.). Vanguard. https://investor.vanguard.com/investor-resources-education/online-trading

Our best mental health tips - backed by research. (2023). Mentalhealth. https://www.mentalhealth.org.uk/explore-mental-health/publications/our-best-mental-health-tips

Pascale, R. (2019, October 21). *Why It's Important To Stay Social In Retirement And How To Do It*. Forbes. https://www.forbes.com/sites/robpascale/2019/10/31/staying-social-in-retirement/?sh=596f28f8779b

Passive income ideas: 15 strategies for beginners. (n.d.). Shopify. https://www.shopify.com/za/blog/passive-income-ideas

Pisani, B. (2022, October 3). *Billionaire Warren Buffett swears by this inexpensive investing strategy that anyone can try*. CNBC. https://www.cnbc.com/2022/10/03/billionaire-warren-buffett-swears-by-this-inexpensive-investing-strategy-that-anyone-can-try.html

Planning for pre-retirement. (n.d.). Active Super. https://www.activesuper.com.au/news-and-events/blog/planning-for-pre-retirement/

Planning to retire within 10 years? These 7 steps could help you get ready. (n.d.). Merrill Edge. https://www.merrilledge.com/article/7-steps-prepare-for-your-upcoming-retirement

Pritchard, J. (2020, November 8). *12 Retirement Questions to Ask, Answers by a CFP® Professional.* Approach Financial. https://www.approachfp.com/retirement-questions-to-ask/

RAJ, D. (2023, April 5). *20 Quotes about Health is Wealth to Inspire Healthy Living.* Find Insights. https://findinsights.in/quotes-about-health-is-wealth/

Retirees who are working part-time: is it because you need the money or because you want to stay active? (2013). Reddit. https://www.reddit.com/r/retirement/comments/150stjg/retirees_who_are_working_parttime_is_it_because/

Retirement accounts you should consider. (2023, Feb. 08). U.S. News & World Report. https://money.usnews.com/money/retirement/articles/retirement-accounts-you-should-consider

Retirement calculator - How much money do you need to retire? (n.d.). NerdWallet. https://www.nerdwallet.com/calculator/retirement-calculator

Retirement planning. (2018, August 28). The New York Times.

https://www.nytimes.com/guides/business/savin
g-money-for-retirement

Retirement Stages. (n.d.). Second Wind Movement.
https://secondwindmovement.com/retirement-
stages/

Robinson, L. (2019). *Healthy Eating*. HelpGuide.org.
https://www.helpguide.org/articles/healthy-
eating/healthy-eating.htm

Royal, J. (2022, June 23). *14 Passive Income Ideas To
Help You Make Money In 2021*. Bankrate.
https://www.bankrate.com/investing/passive-
income-
ideas/ps://www.bankrate.com/investing/passive-
income-ideas/

Royal, J. (2022a, June 1). *9 best retirement plans in
February 2024*. Bankrate.
https://www.bankrate.com/retirement/best-
retirement-plans/

Royal, J. (2024, January 2). *What Is A Solo 401(k)?*
Bankrate.
https://www.bankrate.com/retirement/solo-
401k/

S&P 500 Index - 90 Year Historical Chart. (2009).
Macrotrends.net.
https://www.macrotrends.net/2324/sp-500-
historical-chart-data

Schwab Intelligent Portfolios. (n.d.). *Our robo-advisor
does the work, so you don't have to.* Charles

Schwab. https://www.schwab.com/intelligent-portfolios

Schwantes, M. (n.d.). *Five simple exercises to find your life purpose*. Incafrica. https://www.incafrica.com/library/marcel-schwantes-five-simple-exercises-to-find-your-life-purpose

Seagal, T. (2024, February 15). *What Is a Solo 401(k) or Self-Employed 401(k)? Contribution Limit*. Investopedia. https://www.investopedia.com/ask/answers/100314/do-i-need-employer-set-401k-plan.asp

SEP IRA. (n.d.). Charles Schwab. https://www.schwab.com/small-business-retirement-plans/sep-ira

Seven common side hustle mistakes to avoid. (n.d.). OnDeck. https://www.ondeck.com/resources/common-side-hustle-mistakes

Seven tips to maintain social connections in retirement. (2017, May 22). U.S. News & World Report. https://money.usnews.com/money/retirement/aging/articles/2017-05-22/7-tips-to-maintain-social-connections-in-retirement

Siberski, J, MS, CMC. (2010). *The disenchantment phase of retirement, 3(2), 5*. Today's Geriatric Medicine. https://www.todaysgeriatricmedicine.com/archive/050310p5.shtml

Side hustle success stories. (2023, September 23). Vital Dollar. https://vitaldollar.com/side-hustle-success-stories/

Simplified employee pension (SEP) IRA. (n.d.). Vanguard. https://investor.vanguard.com/accounts-plans/small-business-retirement-plans/sep-ira

Six ways to get ready for retirement. (2023, May 05). U.S. Bank Financial IQ. https://www.usbank.com/financialiq/plan-your-future/retirement/6-ways-to-get-ready-for-retirement.html

Slogans on healthy food. (2024, February 05). StyleCraze. https://www.stylecraze.com/articles/slogans-on-healthy-food/

Smart goals for retirement planning. (n.d.). Private Wealth Systems. https://pfswm.com/smart-goals-for-retirement-planning

Social life after retirement. (n.d.). Second Wind Movement. https://secondwindmovement.com/social-life-after-retirement/

Speights, K. (2023, September 10). *Here's How Warren Buffett's Favorite Index Fund Could Help Make You a Milliionaire.* Nasdaq.com. https://www.nasdaq.com/articles/heres-how-warren-buffetts-favorite-index-fund-could-help-make-you-a-milliionaire

Suresh, M. (n.d.-b). *5 Ways to Track Your Expenses.* Moneyview. https://moneyview.in/blog/how-to-track-your-finances/

Suttie, J. (2014, March 14). *How social connections keep seniors healthy.* Greater Good. https://greatergood.berkeley.edu/article/item/how_social_connections_keep_seniors_healthy

Tech safety tips for seniors. (n.d.). Verve Senior Living. https://verveseniorliving.com/news-events-blog/tech-safety-tips-seni

Technology in senior living: Statistics. (n.d.). Zipdo. https://zipdo.co/statistics/technology-in-senior-living/

The 5 stages of retirement everyone will go through. (n.d.). Wild Pine Residence. https://wildpineresidence.ca/the-5-stages-of-retirement-everyone-will-go-through/

The beauty of the solo 401(k) and why everyone should consider one. (2020). Reddit. https://www.reddit.com/r/financialindependence/comments/i1bcd5/the_beauty_of_the_solo_401k_and_why_everyone/

The honeymoon phase of retirement. (n.d.). Physician on FIRE. https://www.physicianonfire.com/honeymoon-phase-of-retirement/

The honeymoon phase of retirement: What No One Else Will Tell You. (2023, Feb. 15.). TOak Pensions. https://www.blog.oakpensions.com/post/the-honeymoon-phase-of-retirement-what-no-one-else-will-tell-you

The importance of an emergency fund. (n.d.). Willful. https://www.willful.co/blog/importance-of-an-emergency-fund

The importance of social interaction for seniors. (2021, July 27). The Legacy of Farmington. https://thelegacyoffarmington.com/the-importance-of-social-interaction-for-seniors/

The Investopedia Team. (2023, July 27). *Simplified employee pension (SEP).* Investopedia. https://www.investopedia.com/terms/s/sep.asp

The Investopedia Team. (2023, September 18.). *Warren Buffett: the oracle of Omaha.* Investopedia. https://www.investopedia.com/warren-buffett-4689826

The journey through the 5 stages of retirement. (n.d.). Inspired Villages. https://www.inspiredvillages.co.uk/blog/the-journey-through-the-5-stages-of-retirement

The math behind saving for retirement. (2019, April 25). Business Insider. https://www.businessinsider.com/personal-finance/retirement-savings-start-at-25-vs-35-2019-4

The Smart Money Manager | Save. Invest. Retire. (2017). Betterment. https://www.betterment.com/

The Source for Seniors. (n.d.). *Tackling tech: Tips for using technology for seniors*. AAAWM. https://www.aaawm.org/article/tackling-tech-tips-for-using-technology-for-seniors

Thirteen quotes to help plan for retirement. (2020, June 25). The Motley Fool. https://www.fool.com/retirement/2020/06/25/13-quotes-to-help-plan-for-retirement.aspx

Thirteen technology tips for seniors: promoting digital connection. (n.d.). Senior Services of America. https://seniorservicesofamerica.com/blog/13-technology-tips-for-seniors-promoting-digital-connection/

Thirty quotes about human interaction that will make you love call center services. (2019, July 18). SAS Call Center. https://www.sascallcenter.com/30-quotes-about-human-interaction-that-will-make-you-love-call-center-services/

Thirty-three best social connection quotes. (2020, October 16). Visible Network Labs. https://visiblenetworklabs.com/2020/10/16/thirty-three-best-social-connection-quotes/

This simple rule has reduced my impulse purchases. (2021, November 20.). The Motley Fool. https://www.fool.com/the-ascent/personal-finance/articles/this-simple-rule-has-reduced-my-impulse-purchases/

Thompson, V. (2020, July 17). *Famous Quotes on Socializing and Well-Being*. Center for the

Advancement of Well-Being. https://wellbeing.gmu.edu/famous-quotes-on-socializing-and-well-being/

Three ways bad health can ruin your retirement. (2019, September 26). The Motley Fool. https://www.fool.com/retirement/2019/09/26/3-ways-bad-health-can-ruin-your-retirement.aspx

Tips for better sleep. (2022, September 13d.). CDC. https://www.cdc.gov/sleep/about_sleep/sleep_hygiene.html

Tips for tracking your expenses. (n.d.). Take Charge America. https://www.takechargeamerica.org/tips-for-tracking-your-expenses/

Together we are beating cancer. (n.d.). *30 fun ways to exercise.* Cancer Research UK. https://www.cancerresearchuk.org/get-involved/find-an-event/the-exercise-challenge/30-ways-to-exercise

Traditional IRA. (n.d.). Vanguard. https://investor.vanguard.com/accounts-plans/iras/traditional-ira

Traditional IRA. (n.d.). *What is a traditional IRA?* Charles Schwab. https://www.schwab.com/ira/traditional-ira

Twenty fun ways to exercise: stay active and healthy. (n.d.). Physio Tattva. https://www.physiotattva.com/blog/20-fun-ways-to-exercise-stay-active-and-healthy

Types of Retirement Plans. (2023, May 5). *Internal Revenue Service.* Irs.gov. https://www.irs.gov/retirement-plans/plan-sponsor/types-of-retirement-plans

Types of retirement plans. (n.d.). U.S. Department of Labor. https://www.dol.gov/general/topic/retirement/typesofplans

Vil, J.-P. (2023, March 23). *Retirement advice: How to beat the retirement blues.* HealthPartners Blog. https://www.healthpartners.com/blog/retirement-stages-and-how-to-beat-retirement-depression/

Warren Buffett quotes. (n.d.). AZ Quotes. https://www.azquotes.com/quote/1095350?ref=index-funds

Warren Buffett. (2024, February 21). Forbes. https://www.forbes.com/profile/warren-buffett/?sh=2239dc8e4639

Weiss, P. (2021a, June 9). *How Do You Decide Where to Live When You Retire?* Apprise Wealth Management. https://apprisewealth.com/news/how-do-you-decide-where-to-live-when-you-retire/

Wellbeing | Mind, the mental health charity - help for mental health problems. (2019). Mind. https://www.mind.org.uk/information-support/tips-for-everyday-living/wellbeing/

Wells, L. (2023, September 26). *15 Part-Time Jobs For Retirees.* Bankrate.

https://www.bankrate.com/retirement/part-time-jobs-for-retirees/

Were you ever bored in retirement? (2013). Reddit. https://www.reddit.com/r/AskOldPeople/comments/16nud6h/were_you_ever_bored_in_retirement/

Wetzel, A. (2023, October 12). *7 reasons why Warren Buffett thinks you should be an index investor.* Justetf. https://www.justetf.com/en/academy/warren-buffett-index-investor.html

What are the five stages of retirement? (n.d.). Caring Places Management. https://www.caringplaces.com/what-are-the-five-stages-of-retirement/

What are the five stages of retirement? (n.d.). Ohio Presbyterian Retirement Services (OPRS). https://www.oprs.org/what-are-the-five-stages-of-retirement/

What is a 401(k)? (2024, February 13). NerdWallet. https://www.nerdwallet.com/article/investing/what-is-a-401k

What is a Retirement Vision Board? (2022, December 20). InLife. https://www.insularlife.com.ph/articles/what-is-a-retirement-vision-board-00000260

What is a robo-advisor? (n.d.). Schwab. https://www.schwab.com/automated-investing/what-is-a-robo-advisor

What is a SEP IRA? (2023, November 02.). NerdWallet. https://www.nerdwallet.com/article/investing/what-is-a-sep-ira

What is a solo 401(k)? (2024, January 04.). NerdWallet. https://www.nerdwallet.com/article/investing/what-is-a-solo-401k

What is a traditional IRA? (2023, November 02.). NerdWallet. https://www.nerdwallet.com/article/investing/what-is-a-traditional-ira

What is an index fund? (n.d.). Vanguard. https://investor.vanguard.com/investor-resources-education/understanding-investment-types/what-is-an-index-fund

What is your side hustle? (2015). Reddit. https://www.reddit.com/r/sidehustle/comments/155x7a9/what_is_your_side_hustle/

What were your most life changing diet changes? (2020). Reddit. https://www.reddit.com/r/nutrition/comments/julnzf/what_were_your_most_life_changing_diet_changes/

When can I retire? (2023, November 09.). The Motley Fool. https://www.fool.com/retirement/strategies/when-can-i-retire/

Where Will You Live in Retirement? (2022, July 26). Retire Successfully. https://retiresuccessfully.co.za/where-will-you-live-in-retirement/

Why Warren Buffett recommends Exchange Traded Funds (ETFs). (2020, March 18). Action to Healthy Wealthy.

www.ingramcontent.com/pod-product-compliance
Lightning Source LLC
Chambersburg PA
CBHW030503210326
41597CB00013B/772